COUNTRY HERB COOKING

COUNTRY HERB COOKING

Four Seasons of Recipes from Pickity Place

JUDY WALTER

This edition published in 1993 by
HERB FARM PRESS
c/o Pickity Place
Nutting Hill Road
Mason, NH 03048

Produced by The Triangle Group, Ltd.
118 East 25th Street
New York, NY 10010

Design: Tony Meisel
Drawings: Patience Webb

Printed in the United States of America

ISBN 0-944297-15-3

CONTENTS

What was paradise?
But a garden.
An orchard of trees and herbs,
Full of pleasure, and nothing
there but delights.

William Lawson

SEPTEMBER

JANUARY

Wassail Song
Oh here we come a-wassailing
among the leaves so green
here we come awandering
so fair to be seen.
Love and joy come to you
and to you a wassail too
and God bless you and send you
a Happy New Year
and God send you a Happy New Year.

Epiphany, or "Little Christmas" is the time when the Wise Men arrived in Bethlehem to pay homage to the Holy Child. In parts of rural England, ancient farm festivals have combined with Christian symbolism. Cider is poured around the roots of fruit trees, and cider-soaked cakes are placed in the branches. A song is sung to the trees – "hats full, caps full, three-score baskets full, and all our pockets full too." This is called "Wassailing the trees," to assure the triumph of the coming warm spring over the current cold weather.

Janus, in Roman mythology, was a God who had two faces – one which looked into the past and the other into the future. Janus served as the God of gates and doors. His name comes from the Latin Janua, meaning gate. January, the first month of the year, was named for Janus. The turn of the year is a time for omens and superstitions; for turning away from the old year and facing the new. The first person to cross the threshold on New Year's Day indicates the sort of fortune the household may expect in the coming year.

The ancient and pagan figure of Old Father Time, complete with sickle and the sands of time running out, traditionally represents the dying year. The sentiment of "Auld Lang Syne" is in tune with the ancient belief that at the New Year ancestors return to the family hearth.

January's sun is weak, and icicles hang from the roof, many of them three feet long! We will use some of these for freezing homemade ice cream. Snow is piling up and the red Jeep with its plow is getting its exercise.

Temperatures plunge to zero and below, and we hope the tender roots in the earth are warm enough. When a warmer day is forecast, we sneak out for a day of skiing. Holiday decorations have been packed away for another year, and in the dining room, silver stars hang in the windows. Framed woodcut prints embellish the walls, and on the mantle champagne glasses are bubbling over with "frothy" ribbons.

This is our first time for a rest after many busy months, and we take full advantage!

THYME

Perennial
thymus vulgaris

A first step into the garden reveals a look at thyme. Legend tells us that thyme tea was thought to prevent shyness. I always encourage those with me on a garden tour to nibble a bit of the tasty leaf so that questions are freely forthcoming, and shyness does not prevail!

Thymus was Greek for "courage." A bed of thyme was once thought to be home to fairies, and gardener's set aside a patch for them. Thyme pillows were thought to relieve melancholy.

Bees love the tiny thyme blossoms – take care when weeding this plant! It makes an ideal edging plant and is available in varieties with pink, lavender, crimson or white flowers. Thyme makes an excellent windowsill herb.

Thymus vulgaris, often called common or culinary thyme, this variety is best for seasoning. It has upright growth, woody stems and grows to about twelve inches in height. Its leaves are narrow and may vary from dark green to grey green. These small, shrubby hedges make an attractive border in the garden.

Thymus serpyllum, called creeping or mother-of-thyme, makes an excellent ground cover. The creeping thymes are excellent for rock gardens, and are sturdy enough to be planted among the bricks in a pathway.

There are scores of thymes to choose from in planning your garden. Some are silver or gold leafed, and many are named for the color of their tiny blossom, such as crimson thyme. *Thymus citriodorus*, lemon thyme, will delight you with it s rich lemon-scented leaves. It is a wonderful taste enhancer for chicken or fish dishes. Lemon thyme is not as hardy as some other varieties, and propagation by cuttings or root divisions is best to insure a strongly fragrant plant.

Common thyme grows readily from seed, and others can be propagated by division or cuttings. It needs no fertilizing. Plant in a well-drained, sunny location in light, sandy soil. It is wise to mulch your thyme plants during winter months in cold climates.

Thyme leaves should be harvested just as the flower buds are beginning to open. Hang in bunches or lay on screens in a dry, shady location. Store in an airtight jar. Dried thyme becomes very pungent.

Plant thyme near eggplant, potatoes and tomatoes. It is also recommended to repel whiteflies and cabbageworms. Thyme plants which look winter-killed are often only damaged and will recover. Leave at least three inches above ground in the fall.

The flavor of thyme blends well with lemon, garlic and basil. For a new taste, try flavored varieties such as lemon thyme or nutmeg, oregano or caraway thyme. Thyme-flavored honey is a favorite. A few leaves of this evergreen plant add a special taste treat to soups, stews and casseroles. Thyme makes a delicious herb butter; try it on corn on the cob!

Thyme is an important ingredient in our Herbs for Chicken and Fish, Bouquet Garni, and in stuffing mixtures. Thyme tea is a delicious winter brew, and was once believed to prevent nightmares! Thyme lends good flavor to red meat, poultry and fish. It is a delicious vegetable enhancer, but a strong one; in most cases a "pinch of thyme" is enough!

Thyme vinegar, after steeping in the sun for several weeks, is useful in treating insect bites and stings. Thymol, the oil derived from the fresh leaves of thyme, is a powerful antiseptic and is found today among disinfectants. You will find thyme used in cosmetics, mouthwash, and toothpaste. Thyme is also useful as a moth preventive in closets and drawers.

FOR POULTRY STUFFING

Blend together:
1 tablespoon lemon thyme
2 tablespoons sage
1 tablespoon lovage
1 tablespoon parsley

VEGETABLE CHOWDER

1/2 cup chopped celery
1 8 oz. can evaporated milk
2 cups sliced cooked potatoes
2 cups lima beans
2 cups creamed corn
1 medium onion, diced
2 tablespoons butter
1/2 teaspoon dried thyme

Cook the onions and celery in the butter until transparent.
Combine all the ingredients, heat and serve. Garnish with
a sprig of fresh thyme.

HERB CHEESE SPREAD

1 teaspoon fresh thyme
1 teaspoon fresh chives
1 teaspoon fresh sage
1 clove garlic, crushed
1 8-ounce package cream cheese, softened
1/2 cup sour cream

Blend all ingredients well and serve with crackers.

SUMMER SQUASH CASSEROLE

6 cups sliced summer squash
1/2 cup onion, chopped
1 10 3/4-ounce can cream of chicken soup
1 cup sour cream
1 cup shredded carrots
1/2 teaspoon dried thyme
1 8-ounce package herb stuffing mix
1/2 cup butter, melted

Cook the squash and onion in water for 5 minutes, then drain well. Add the sour cream, soup, thyme and carrots. Combine the stuffing mix and the butter. Spread half the stuffing mixture in a buttered 1 1/2 quart casserole. Add the vegetable mixture and then top with the remaining stuffing. Bake at 350 degrees for 25-30 minutes.

CHICKEN IN THYME BROTH

1 broiler fryer chicken, cut in serving size pieces
2 tablespoons butter
1 green pepper, cut in strips
1 teaspoon dried thyme
1/2 teaspoon paprika
1 medium onion, sliced
1/2 cup celery, chopped
1 16 ounce can tomatoes
1 4 ounce can mushrooms

Sprinkle the chicken pieces with the paprika. Melt the butter in a large skillet and brown the chicken on all sides. Add the onion, green pepper, celery, tomatoes, and thyme. Bring to a boil and cover. Reduce the heat and simmer for 20 minutes. Add the mushrooms (with juice). Simmer 5-10 minutes more.

FISH CASSEROLE WITH LEMON THYME

3 cups cooked, flaked fish (cod, sole or flounder are good choices)
2 tablespoons fresh lemon thyme, chopped
1 tablespoon fresh parsley, chopped
1 1/2 cups white sauce
freshly ground pepper
breadcrumbs
butter

Prepare the white sauce and add the fish and the herbs. Pour into a casserole dish, top with bread crumbs and a few bits of butter. Heat at 350 degrees for 15 minutes.

LEMON THYME CHICKEN WITH GARLIC

4 chicken breasts, skin and bones removed
2 tablespoons extra virgin olive oil
3 large cloves garlic, crushed
2 tablespoons fresh lemon thyme, chopped
2 tablespoons fresh oregano, chopped
Freshly ground black pepper
1/2 cup water

Rub the chicken breasts with the oil, garlic, herbs and pepper and set aside for 3 hours allowing the flavors to develop. Place prepared chicken in a heavy skillet, add water and cover. Cook over low heat for 10 to 12 minutes, turning once, until chicken is browned outside and done in the center. Serve with rice to catch the herb juices.

THYME BOUILLON

2 quarts chicken broth
1 cup dry white wine
2 stalks diced celery
1 onion, diced
1 large carrot, diced
1 tablespoon fresh parsley
4 sprigs fresh thyme
2 bay leaves
12 peppercorns
2 cloves
1 clove garlic
1 tablespoon lemon juice

Simmer all together for 30 minutes. Remove bay leaves.

MEATBALLS STROGANOFF

1 pound ground beef
3/4 pound ground pork
1 cup cracker crumbs
2 teaspoons salt
dash pepper
1/2 teaspoon thyme, dried
1/2 teaspoon oregano, dried
1/2 cup milk
2 eggs
1 1/2 cup sour cream
1/2 cup sour cream
1 1/3 cups sliced mushrooms

Combine all ingredients except sour cream and mushrooms and form into meatballs. Bake on greased cookie sheet for 20 minutes at 375 degrees. Drain the excess fat, transfer to saucepan and add the 1 1/2 cups sour cream. Cover and simmer 1 hour. Remove meatballs to warm serving dish. Stir 1/2 cup sour cream into the mixture in the skillet; add mushrooms. Heat to boiling and pour over the meatballs.

CHICKEN TURNOVERS WITH SAGE AND THYME

1 1/2 recipes of your favorite pie pastry*
2 tablespoons oil
2 pounds chicken, cubed
1/4 cup sherry
1/2 cup chicken bouillon
1/2 teaspoon dried thyme
1/2 teaspoon dried sage
1 medium onion, chopped
3 tart apples, peeled and diced
applesauce and cinnamon

Brown the chicken in the oil. Stir in the sherry and cook
2 minutes. Drain all liquid. Add the broth and herbs. Simmer,
covered, for 1/2 hour until chicken is tender. Add onions and
simmer 5 minutes longer. Add apples and cook 10 minutes.
Cool. Roll pastry 1/2" thick. Cut out 7" round circles. Beat
1 egg with 1 tablespoon milk and moisten edges with this. Put
1/2 cup filling on each round and fold over to form a half circle.
Crimp edges and glaze the pies with the egg wash. Cut 3 slits in
the top of each pie. Place on ungreased baking sheet. Bake at
350 degrees for 25 minutes or until browned. Serve with hot
applesauce sprinkled with cinnamon.

*Pastry for Chicken Turnovers

2 1/2 cups sifted all-purpose flour
1 teaspoon salt
2 teaspoons celery seed
8 tablespoons (1 stick) unsalted, cold butter, cut into pieces
6 tablespoons vegetable shortening
5-6 tablespons ice water

Combine, flour and salt. Add the celery seed and mix well. Add the butter and shortening and work with a pastry blender until mixture resembles coarse crumbs. Sprinkle the ice water over the mixture 2 tablespoons at a time and toss after each addition. Gather the dough into a ball, wrap in wax paper and chill for 30 minutes.

GLAZED ONIONS

12 onions, boiled
4 tablespoons butter
2 tablespoons honey
1/2 teaspoon salt
1 teaspoon dried thyme

Arrange the boiled onions in a buttered baking dish in one layer. Melt the butter and add the honey and thyme. Cook and stir until honey is liquid. Pour over the onions to coat them. Bake at 400 degrees about 25 minutes. Baste the onions from time to time so they will be golden brown.

SPANISH BROWN RICE

1 onion, diced
1 red pepper, diced
2 cloves garlic, minced
6 ripe tomatoes, cut into pieces
2 1/2 cups brown rice, uncooked
4 cups boiling water

Saute onion, pepper and garlic until brown in a large non-stick frying pan. Add small amounts of water to keep vegetables from sticking, then mix in the tomatoes and bring to a boil. Stir in the rice and boiling water and tightly cover the pan. Lower heat and cook until water is absorbed, approximately 40 minutes.

VEGETARIAN CASSEROLE

1 tablespoon vegetable oil
1 small onion, diced
1 stalk celery, diced
1/2 cup sliced mushrooms
1/2 cup chopped broccoli
1/2 cup sliced carrots
1/2 cup green beans
1/2 cup zucchini, diced
1 tablespoon Fines Herbes
3 cups cooked rice
1 pint sour cream
6 ounces mozzarella cheese

Saute the vegetables in hot oil until tender. In a casserole dish, mix the cooked vegetables with the cooked rice and the herbs. Spread sour cream over the top. Arrange mozzarella strips over the sour cream. Bake at 350 degrees till hot and the cheese is melted.

A MENU FOR JANUARY

Herby Stuffed Mushrooms

Onion Cheddar Soup

Whole Wheat Spice Bread

Mixed Greens with Herbed Salad Dressing

Beef Bourguignon

Broccoli with Orange Thyme Sauce

Buttermilk Clove Cake

HERBY STUFFED MUSHROOMS

15 large mushrooms, cleaned
1 10-ounce package frozen spinach, chopped
1 cup low-fat cottage cheese
2 cloves garlic, minced
2 tablespoons parsley leaves
1 teaspoon onion powder
1/2 teaspoon thyme
1/2 teaspoon dill weed
1/8 teaspoon nutmeg

Remove the stems from the mushrooms and finely chop them.
Dip the mushroom caps in melted butter and place them on a
cookie sheet. In a food processor puree the spinach, cottage
cheese, garlic and herbs. Combine with the chopped stems and
stuff the mushrooms generously. Bake at 425 degrees for 12 to
15 minutes. Serve immediately, garnished with a lemon wedge.

ONION-CHEDDAR SOUP

4 onions
6 tablespoons butter
4 cups hot water
2 cups hot water
10 ounces grated cheddar cheese
1/2 cup soy sauce

Simmer the onions and butter until golden brown. Add 4 cups
of hot water. In a blender mix 2 cups hot water and cheddar
cheese. Add the blended mixture to the onions. Add the soy
sauce and heat.

WHOLE WHEAT SPICE BREAD

2 cups scalded milk
1/4 cup brown sugar
1 teaspoon salt
1/4 cup honey
1/3 cup soft butter
1/3 cup orange juice
2 packages dry yeast
1/4 cup warm water
1 egg
2 1/2 cups white flour
4 cups whole wheat flour
1/2 teaspoon cumin seed

Pour the scalded milk over the brown sugar, salt, honey and butter. Cool until lukewarm, then add the orange juice. Dissolve the yeast in the water and let stand 5 minutes. Add to the milk mixture along with the egg, and blend well. Stir in the white flour and beat until smooth. Add the whole wheat flour and the cumin seed. Turn the dough out and knead until smooth and elastic. Place in a buttered bowl, cover, and let rise for 30 minutes. Shape into 2 loaves and place in buttered 9" loaf pans. cover and let rise again. Bake at 425 degrees for 10 minutes, then at 350 degrees for 25-30 minutes longer. Brush the tops of the hot loaves with melted butter.

MIXED GREENS WITH HERBED SALAD DRESSING

2/3 cup tarragon vinegar
1/2 cup safflower oil
1/3 cup extra virgin olive oil
2 teaspoons mayonnaise
3 cloves garlic, minced
1 teaspoon Dijon mustard
1 teaspoon thyme
1/2 teaspoon tarragon

Combine all ingredients in a jar and shake well. Store, tightly covered, in the refrigerator until ready to use. Shake well and serve over assorted fresh greens.

BEEF BOURGUIGNON

2 1/2 pounds boneless beef chuck
2 tablespoons butter
3 tablespoons brandy
1/2 pound small white onions, peeled
1/2 pound small fresh mushrooms
2 1/2 tablespoons arrowroot
2 tablespoons tomato paste
1 1/2 cups burgundy
3/4 cups dry sherry
3/4 cup port
1 10-ounce can condensed beef broth
1/8 teaspoon pepper
1 bay leaf
chopped parsley

Cut the beef into 1 1/2 inch cubes. Brown in a Dutch oven over high heat. In a small saucepan, heat brandy and pour it over the beef. Remove the beef and set aside. Add butter to Dutch oven and heat slightly. Add onions and cook slightly. Add the mushrooms and cook, stirring, for 3 minutes. Remove onions and mushrooms. Remove Dutch oven from heat. Using a wooden spoon, stir in the arrowroot and tomato paste until well blended. Stir in the burgundy, sherry, port and beef broth. Preheat oven to 350 degrees. Bring the wine mixture just to boiling, stirring. Remove from heat. Add the beef, pepper, bay leaf, onions, mushrooms, and remaining brandy. Mix well. Cover and bake, stirring occasionally for 1 1/2 hours. Garnish with fresh parsley.

BROCCOLI WITH ORANGE THYME SAUCE

5 cups broccoli in serving size spears
2 3-ounce packages cream cheese
1/4 cup milk
1/2 teaspoon grated orange peel
1/4 teaspoon thyme, dried
1/4 cup orange juice
3 tablespoons chopped walnuts

Cook the broccoli until crisp-tender, 10-12 minutes. In a small saucepan combine the cream cheese, milk, orange peel and thyme. Cook over medium heat, stirring, until smooth. Add orange juice and mix well. Serve the sauce over the broccoli, garnished with chopped nuts and orange slices.

BUTTERMILK CLOVE CAKE

3 cups flour
1 1/2 teaspoon baking soda
2 teaspoon ground cloves
1 teaspoon ground cinnamon
1/2 teaspoon ground nutmeg
1/4 teaspoon ground allspice
1 cup butter, softened
1 1/2 cups light brown sugar, packed
2 eggs
1 egg yolk
1 1/2 cups buttermilk
Nut Filling
Butter Frosting

Sift flour with baking soda and spices. In a large bowl, beat butter, brown sugar, eggs and egg yolk at high speed about 5 minutes. At low speed beat in the flour mixture in fourths, alternately with the buttermilk (in thirds). Beat 1 minute only. Pour batter into 2 greased and floured 9" round layer pans. Bake at 350 degrees 25-30 minutes. Cool in pans 10 minutes, then remove and cool completely.

Nut Filling:
1/2 cup sugar
1/2 cup water
1 1/2 cups ground walnuts
1 teaspoon vanilla extract

In small saucepan combine sugar and water. Bring to a boil, stirring until sugar is dissolved. Stir in walnuts. Cook 5 minutes, just until mixture thickens slightly. Remove and add vanilla. Cool completely, then spread between layers.

Butter Frosting:
1/2 cups butter
3 cups confectioner's sugar, sifted
4 tablespoons cream or evaporated milk
1 teaspoon vanilla extract

Cream the butter. Add remaining ingredients and continue creaming until mixture is well blended and fluffy.

FEBRUARY

"Good morrow!"
Tis St. Valentine's Day
All in the morning betime
And I a maid at your window
To be your Valentine!

William Shakespeare

Although the month of February is still chill with winter's cold, it promises the spring to come. Rejoice in the season of love! The old-fashioned valentine includes many meaningful symbols. The ribbon and lace frills are associated with the days of knighthood when a man in armor wore a ribbon given him by his lady love. Cupid is one of the gods of mythology whose Latin name means desire. The rose is the most loved flower the world over, and, if rearranged, the letters spell "Eros" the god of love. The doves are birds which mate for life, thus symbolizing fidelity.

Symbols of love include the love knot. The two circles intertwined, side by side represent affection without beginning and without end. When it is fashioned from gold, it signifies eternal love.

Many foods are thought to stimulate affection; these "foods of love" include various meats, fish, fruits and wines. Fruits that have seeds are considered important foods of love. The apple has been associated with love since the Garden of Eden.

There are certain herbs that are thought to cool and quiet the emotions. These include fennel, chicory and rue!

Southernwood is known as the passion herb. It is also known by two other names: "Lad's Love" and "Maiden's Ruin!"

Seed catalogs have started arriving and we are dreaming and planning ahead. Lists are made and remade, and ideas for new gardens begin to unfold in our thoughts. We take inventory in the greenhouse, and plan for the thousands of new seedlings soon to appear. Winter birds fly in and out of feeders, and the fat grey squirrel tries in vain to steal some of their bounty!

A Valentine box, decorated with lace and red hearts, sits on the old Parson's Bench, and Victorian cards with sayings of love grace the mantle. A friend has brought us a beautiful, heart-shaped wreath fashioned from heather.

We heap on more wood, sip a cup of steaming spice tea, and think about ideas for new herbal products. We explore the markets, looking for new and exciting items to offer our customers. "If winter comes, can spring be far behind?"

OREGANO

Hardy Perennial
origanum vulgare

Oregano's name means "joy of the mountain", derived from the Greek oros, meaning "mountain", and ganos, meaning "joy". Many of oregano's early uses were medicinal; the Greeks used the leaves for making poultices which were thought to relieve scorpion and spider bites! Oil of oregano was once used to ease an aching tooth, and, when mixed with olive oil, was rubbed into balding scalps!

Oregano, also called wild marjoram, grows to two feet with grey-green oval leaves. Its flowers vary in color from pink to purple or white. It prefers good drainage, full sun and average soil. Seeds will grow readily, or propagate by division of established plants in the spring. It can become very invasive in the garden, so discipline it!

The *o. heracleoticum*, or Greek oregano has the finest flavor of the two varieties. The plant has a white flower, very hairy leaves, and is not hardy in our area. It will winter over if brought inside and is very attractive in a hanging pot. Harvest the plant as the flowers appear and dry them in bunches.

Oregano is a strong tasting herb, and becomes more pungent when it is dried. An essential ingredient in spaghetti, pizza, and tomato dishes, it goes equally well with eggplant and zucchini. Try sprinkling it on beef or lamb before cooking.

TOMATO SALAD WITH OREGANO

Line a salad bowl with fresh greens. Alternate slices of ripe tomato, sliced red onion rings and thinly sliced mozzarella cheese. Add chopped fresh oregano leaves and drizzle with olive oil.

BASIC TOMATO SAUCE

1/2 cup finely chopped onion
1 tablespoon olive oil
2/3 cup water
2 1/2 cups coarsely chopped fresh tomatoes
1 clove garlic, peeled and crushed
1 teaspoon sugar
1 bay leaf
1 teaspoon dried oregano
1 teaspoon dried basil
1/2 teaspoon dried summer savory

Sauté the onions in the olive oil until they are transparent. Add the water and stir well. Add the tomatoes, garlic, sugar and the herbs. Bring to a boil, stirring constantly, then lower the heat and simmer for 30 minutes. Remove the bay leaf. Run the sauce through a strainer and reheat before serving. Use the sauce with pasta or as a pizza topping.

ITALIAN VEGETABLE SOUP

1/4 pound mushrooms, sliced
3 garlic cloves, minced
2 onions, chopped
2 tablespoons oil
1 teaspoon basil, dried
1 tablespoon oregano, dried
2 bay leaves
pinch of thyme
1/4 teaspoon black pepper
3 cups crushed tomatoes
1 teaspoon honey
1/4 cup white wine
2 tablespoons tamari sauce
2 cups chicken broth
2 cups drained, cooked kidney beans
1 zucchini, finely sliced
1 can corn, drained
1 large green pepper
2 tablespoons chopped fresh parsley

Sauté mushrooms, garlic and onions in hot oil. Add seasonings, tomatoes, honey, wine, tamari and chicken broth and simmer for 1 hour. Add the drained beans, corn, zucchini, pepper and parsley and cook until vegetables are tender.

VEGETABLE CASSEROLE

1/2 cup butter
3/4 cup green peppers
2 cloves garlic, crushed
1/4 cup flour
1/4 teaspoon pepper
2 teaspoons dried basil
1 can onions, well drained and chopped
1/3 cup milk
1 1/4 cup grated cheddar cheese
1 can whole tomatoes, well drained
1 can corn, well drained
1 can green beans, well drained
2 teaspoons dried oregano
phyllo

Sauté the peppers and garlic in the butter. Stir in the flour and milk and mix well. Add the spices and stir in the cheese until melted. Add the tomatoes, corn, beans, and onions. Spread out 6 layers of phyllo on a foil lined cookie sheet. Spread with 1/2 the mixture. Roll up, seal and brush the top with melted butter. Make a second roll. Bake at 350 degrees for 40 minutes.

SWEET POTATO CASSEROLE

1 16-ounce can sweet potatoes
1 teaspoon oregano, dried
1/4 cup brown sugar
1/2 cup raisins
1 16-ounce jar applesauce
1 teaspoon caraway seed
1/4 cup sherry
soft breadcrumbs mixed with 1/2 teaspoon cinnamon

Slice the potatoes and arrange them in a casserole. Sprinkle
with the oregano. Cover with the brown sugar and raisins.
Spread with the applesauce and sprinkle on the caraway seed.
Pour on the sherry and top with the spiced breadcrumbs. Bake
at 350 degrees for 30 minutes.

SPINACH AND FETA CHEESE TRIANGLES
WITH OREGANO

1 bag spinach
1 medium onion, minced and sautéed in 3 tablespoons butter
1 10-ounce package feta cheese
1 tablespoon oregano
1/4 teaspoon grated nutmeg
salt and pepper to taste
9 sheets phyllo
1 1/2 sticks melted butter

Wash spinach and cook in 1/4 cup water until wilted. Combine
the cooked spinach, sautéed onions, feta cheese and the spices.
Brush each sheet of phyllo with butter and fold in half lengthwise. Fold in half again and brush with butter. Spoon 2 tablespoons cheese mix on the phyllo and fold forming a triangle.
Bake at 375 degrees on buttered baking sheet for 20 minutes.

MANICOTTI CREPES

1 cup cottage cheese
1 3-ounce package cream cheese, softened
2 tablespoons butter, softened
2 tablespoons chopped fresh parsley
1 egg, beaten
1 tablespoon chopped scallions
8 cooked crepes (see index)
1 15-ounce jar Marinara Sauce
2 teaspoons fresh parsley, chopped
2 teaspoons dried oregano
2 teaspoons dried basil
1/4 teaspoon garlic powder
1/4 cup parmesan cheese

Combine the first six ingredients. Spoon 3 tablespoons of this mixture into the center of each crepe. Combine the sauce with the parsley, oregano, basil and garlic. Place the filled crepes in a shallow baking pan and pour the sauce over them. Sprinkle with parmesan cheese. Bake at 350 degrees for 20-30 minutes.

FRENCH GREEN BEANS IN SAUCE

2 tablespoons butter
1 teaspoon sugar
1 tablespoon dry Lipton Onion Soup Mix
dash pepper
*Herb Buttered Bread Crumbs
1 cup sour cream
5 slices swiss cheese, crumbled
3 cans french style green beans, drained

Mix all ingredients together except beans and crumbs. Stir until smooth. Mix in the beans and pour into a 3-quart casserole. Top with Herb Bread Crumbs. Bake at 325 degrees for 25 minutes.

*Herb Bread Crumbs
1/4 cup butter
1 teaspoon onion powder
1/2 teaspoon basil, dried
1/2 teaspoon chervil, dried
1/2 teaspoon oregano, dried
day old bread, cubed and torn into crumbs

Melt the butter and stir in the onion powder, basil, chervil and oregano. Pour over the bread.

GREEK GREEN BEANS

1/4 cup extra virgin olive oil
3 cloves garlic, minced
1 onion, thinly sliced
1 tablespoon oregano
1 tablespoon basil
1 pound green beans, broken into 1-inch pieces
1 8-ounce can tomato sauce, chunky style

Sauté garlic and onion in olive oil in saucepan until tender but not brown. Add remaining ingredients and simmer until beans are tender, stirring occasionally. Garnish each serving with an oregano flower.

EGGPLANT WITH OREGANO

2 pounds eggplant
4 eggs
2 tablespoons water
2 cups breadcrumbs, crushed
1/2 cup olive oil
3/4 cup grated parmesan cheese
3 teaspoons chopped fresh oregano
1 cup feta cheese
Basic Tomato Sauce (see index)

Peel the eggplant and slice into 1/2" pieces. Beat the eggs with the water. Dip the eggplant into the eggs, then into the crumbs. Sauté the eggplant in 1/4 cup of the olive oil until browned on both sides. Remove and drain on paper towels. Place half the eggplant in a 9" X 13" pan. Sprinkle with 1/3 of the parmesan cheese, 1/3 of the fresh oregano, and 1/3 of the feta cheese. Cover with tomato sauce. Repeat the layers, top with the remaining cheeses. Bake at 350 degrees for 30 minutes.

EGGPLANT DIP

1 medium eggplant cooked, peeled and mashed
1 tomato, peeled and chopped
1 onion, finely chopped
1 clove garlic, minced
1 tablespoon fresh oregano, chopped
1 tablespoon olive oil
1 tablespoon red wine vinegar
grated parmesan cheese

Combine all ingredients except cheese. Spread in a shallow baking dish and sprinkle with cheese. Bake at 350 degrees 15 minutes until hot and cheese is melted.

BAKED CHERRY TOMATOES

2 cups cherry tomatoes
1 tablespoon brown sugar
1 tablespoon fresh oregano, chopped
2 tablespoons olive oil

Place the tomatoes in a baking dish. Sprinkle on the brown sugar and oregano. Pour the oil over all, cover and bake at 350 degrees for about 5 minutes.

HOT POTATO SALAD

1 1/2 pounds new potatoes
2 tablespoons onion, finely chopped
3 tablespoons olive oil
1 tablespoon white wine or herb vinegar
2 tablespoons chopped fresh sweet marjoram

Wash the potatoes and cook them in their skins. Peel if desired, and cut into quarters. Stir in the chopped onion and the marjoram. Combine the oil and vinegar and pour over the hot potatoes. Mix gently.

SHRIMP IN HERB BUTTER

2 cups cooked shrimp
1/2 cup butter
1 onion, chopped
1 clove garlic, crushed
1 teaspoon paprika
1 tablespoon fresh chives, chopped
1 teaspoon fresh basil, chopped
2 teaspoons fresh sweet marjoram, chopped
1/2 teaspoon Worcestershire sauce
3 drops Tabasco

Sauté the onion and garlic in the butter until transparent. Add the paprika, fresh herbs, Worcestershire sauce and the Tabasco. Blend well; stir in the cooked shrimp and simmer to blend the flavors.

HERB FLOUR

2 cups flour
1 teaspoon dried marjoram
1 teaspoon dried thyme
freshly ground pepper

Combine all and store in a jar. Use to stir into sauces and gravies, or when making pastry or biscuits.

PAIN D'EPICES

1 1/2 cups boiling water
3/4 cup honey
1 cup brown sugar
4 cups flour
1 1/2 teaspoon soda
2 teaspoon cinnamon
1/2 teaspoon ground cloves
1/4 cup rum

Pour the boiling water over the honey and sugar. Mix well. Sift the dry ingredients into a large bowl. Add the liquid ingredients to the dry ingredients and blend thoroughly. Stir the rum in last. Pour into a buttered loaf pan and bake at 350 degrees for 1 1/4 hours, or until the bread tests done. Cool thoroughly and wrap tightly to store. Cut into very thin slices and serve with jam.

ONION BUTTER BREAD

1/2 pound softened butter
1/4 cup finely chopped fresh parsley
1/4 cup finely chopped Egyptian onion stalks

Mix all ingredients and blend together. Slice a loaf of crusty bread three-quarters of the way through and spread each slice with the butter. Wrap in aluminum foil and bake at 350 degrees for 15 minutes.

A MENU FOR FEBRUARY

Tangy Herb Dip

Pepper Bread

Potato Soup with Bay and Chives

Watercress Salad

Butter Herb Baked Fish

Honeyed Carrots

Cherry Cottage Pudding with Sauce

TANGY HERB DIP

1 cup cottage cheese
1/4 cups plain yogurt
1 tablespoon chopped fresh parsley
2 teaspoon lemon juice
3 radishes, grated
1/2 teaspoon dill weed, dried
1/2 teaspoon oregano, dried
1 small clove garlic
1/2 teaspoon tamari sauce

Mix the cottage cheese and yogurt together well. Add all the remaining ingredients and blend thoroughly. Serve with pretzels and crackers.

PEPPER BREAD

1 1/2 cups hot water
1 teaspoon salt
3 tablespoons sugar
2 tablespoons bacon fat
2 packages yeast
1/2 cup warm water
1 large egg
5 cups flour
1 teaspoon freshly ground black pepper
1 teaspoon basil, dried
1/4 cups cooked crumbled bacon

Combine the hot water, salt, 2 tablespoons of the sugar and
the bacon fat. Cool. Add the yeast and the remaining 1 tablespoon of sugar to the warm water and stir to dissolve. Combine
the mixtures and add the egg, flour, pepper and basil. Beat
2-3 minutes, until smooth. Add the bacon. Cover and let rise
until doubled. Stir down and beat 2 minutes more. Pour into
2 greased loaf pans. Cover and let rise until batter reaches the
top of the pans. Bake at 400 degrees for 40 minutes.

POTATO SOUP WITH BAY AND CHIVES

6 medium potatoes, unpeeled
3 tablespoons butter
2 medium onions, chopped
2 bay leaves
1/2 teaspoon white pepper
2 cups yogurt (room temperature)
4 tablespoons minced chives for garnish

Steam the potatoes whole until tender. Sauté the onion and bay in the butter. Sprinkle with the pepper. Cover and cook over low heat for 1/2 hour. Remove skins from the potatoes. In the blender, puree the potatoes with the onions, removing the bay leaves first. Return to the saucepan and whisk in the yogurt. Simmer over low heat 15 minutes, stirring occasionally. Garnish with fresh chives.

WATERCRESS SALAD

1 bunch fresh watercress
3 tomatoes, sliced
1/2 cup cream cheese
1/4 cup chopped fresh chives
freshly ground black pepper

Wash the watercress well and pat dry. Lay the tender sprigs on individual plates. Place three slices of tomato in the center. Cut the cheese into squares and roll them in the chopped chives. Place these squares in the center of the salad and pepper.

BUTTER HERB BAKED FISH

1/4 cup grated parmesan cheese
1/2 cup butter
2/3 cup crushed saltine crackers
1/2 teaspoon basil, dried
1/2 teaspoon oregano, dried
1/2 teaspoon salt, if desired
1/4 teaspoon garlic powder
1 pound sole

In a 9" x 13" baking pan melt the butter in preheated oven. Meanwhile, combine the cracker crumbs, parmesan cheese, basil, oregano, salt and garlic. Dip the fish fillet in the butter, then in the crumb mixture. Arrange the fillets in the baking dish. Bake at 350 degrees for 30 minutes or until the fish is tender.

HONEYED CARROTS

5-6 carrots, peeled and cut into 1/2" slices
1/4 cup butter
1/3 cup honey
3 tablespoons freshly chopped parsley
freshly ground pepper

Cook the carrots in boiling water until tender. Melt the butter and add the remaining ingredients. Heat the carrots in the sauce and serve, garnished with more fresh parsley.

CHERRY COTTAGE PUDDING WITH SAUCE

1 No. 2 can pitted red cherries
1/4 cup shortening
2/3 cup sugar
1 egg
1/4 teaspoon almond extract
1 3/4 cups flour
1 teaspoon baking powder
1/2 teaspoon salt
1/2 baking soda
1 cup sour milk

Drain cherries and save juice for sauce. Cream shortening and sugar together until fluffy. Add eggs and flavoring and beat well. Sift flour, baking powder, salt and soda together. Add alternately with milk in small amounts, mixing well after each addition. Add cherries. Pour into buttered 9" square cake pan. Bake at 350 degrees for 45 minutes. Cut into squares and serve with hot *Cherry Sauce.

*Cherry Sauce:
1/4 cup sugar
2 tablespoons flour
1 cup heated red cherry juice
1/4 cup butter
2 tablespoons lemon juice
2 drops almond extract

Combine sugar and flour. Stir in cherry juice gradually, heat to a boil and cook until thickened, stirring constantly. Add butter, lemon juice and extract. Serve hot over cake.

MARCH

Daffodils that come
before the swallow dares
and take the winds of March with
beauty.

Winter's Tale
William Shakespeare

The March winds have arrived – time to savor some of the first delights of spring! Sap flows in the trees, the first pussywillows appear, and hibernating animals leave their winter sleeping places.

There are many superstitions about March. We often hear that "March comes in like a lion and goes out like a lamb." March was the first month on the ancient Roman calendar. Its name honors Mars, the Roman god of war. The early farmers referred to the first three days of March as unlucky. If rain fell on one of these days a poor crop was foretold. Take heed and do not plant seed until March 4!

The vernal equinox takes place on March 20 and 21 and marks the beginning of spring. It is the time when the sun is directly over the equator and day and night are nearly equal all over the earth.

Early spring in New Hampshire begins the sapping season. Cold nights and warm days start the sap flowing in the sugar maples. It takes from 35 to 45 gallons of sap to make one gallon of maple syrup!

Although we know winter is not yet over, a spring thaw has made the road muddy and our fingers itch to feel the earth again.

The first pussywillows are showing us their fuzzy backs, and a few brave snowdrops are blooming in the snow. Soon we will be shearing the sheep, and they will look naked without their warm woolly winter coats. Snow has disappeared in some protected spots, and the Egyptian onions and a few other bold plants are poking their heads above the ground.

The forsythia bushes are loaded with fat buds, and we bring a branch into the warm house to force the blossoms open. In the greenhouse, crocus and daffodils are opening, and soon we will have tulips in full bloom.

The magic of the plant cycle has begun, and trays of minute seedlings are everywhere! We watch and rejoice as they mature and become useful for fragrance, for medicine and for flavoring.

PARSLEY
Hardy Biennial
petroselinum crispum

Curly parsley, usually cultivated as an annual, has bright green curly leaves which make it an excellent border plant.

Italian parsley, *petroselinum hortense*, has a flat leaf and a softer, more preferable flavor for culinary use.

Parsley prefers fertile humus soil and requires a lot of moisture and partial shade. Parsley is very slow to germinate and is said to "go to China and back before it will grow!" In fact, at one time it was believed that only witches could grow it! Don't despair, soaking the seeds in lukewarm water overnight will encourage faster germination. Parsley develops a long taproot and is difficult to transplant.

The foliage of parsley is rich in iron and vitamins and should be harvested as a food and not just used as a garnish. The larger, outer leaves should be cut first, close to the core of the plant leaving no stem.

Parsley can be used to give a sheen to dark hair. Boil 2 tablespoons parsley in 1 pint of water for 20 minutes. Use the strained water as a final rinse.

Parsley can be cut at any time, but must be dried quickly in the oven to keep its flavor and green color. Preheat the oven to 120 degrees and turn it off. Spread parsley heads on a baking sheet and leave in the oven for 15 minutes, turning several times until crisp dry. Keep dried parsley in a tight container, away from any moisture.

Parsley has long been known as a breath freshener and proves that our 20th century use of chlorophyll is not new.

In England, parsley took the place of the stork, and to a small child asking "where did I come from Mommy?" the answer was: "From the parsley bed, my dear!"

The fresh juice of the parsley plant applied to insect stings and bites brings quick relief.

PARSLEY BUTTER

1/2 cup butter
2 tablespoons chopped fresh parsley
1/2 teaspoon lemon juice

Melt the butter. Add the parsley and lemon juice. Mix well and serve with any cooked vegetables. Especially good with carrots or potatoes.

FRIED PARSLEY

1 large bunch fresh parsley
Oil for frying

Wash the parsley and dry thoroughly. Heat the oil in a skillet to 335 degrees. Drop in the sprigs, a few at a time and cook for 3 minutes, turning once. Drain on paper towels and serve at once.

PARSLEY SOUP

1 large onion
2 large carrots
1/4 cup butter
1 large potato, peeled and thinly sliced
3 3/4 cups chicken stock
freshly ground black pepper
3/4 cup fresh Parsley

Slice the onion and carrots very thin, sauté them in the butter for 5 minutes. Add the potato and cook for 3 more minutes. Add the stock and fresh pepper and simmer for 35 minutes. Cool slightly. Puree in a blender with the parsley. Then reheat.

PARSLEY BISCUITS

2 cups flour
3 teaspoons baking powder
1 teaspoon salt
4 tablespoons cold shortening
3/4 cup milk
1 tablespoon fresh parsley, chopped

Sift dry ingredients together and cut in the shortening. Add milk to make a soft dough. Place on a floured board and knead lightly a few seconds. Roll out 1/2" thick and cut with floured biscuit cutter. Bake on greased baking sheet in very hot oven 450 degrees for 12 minutes.

PARSLEY SALAD

2 cups shredded carrots
2 cups chopped celery
4 cups parsley leaves, coarsely chopped
1 dozen radishes, sliced

Toss just to mix, garnish with the radishes when serving.

PARSNIP SOUP

4 tablespoons butter
1 pound parsnips, peeled and cut up
1 cup chopped celery, including leaves
3 cups chicken stock
3 tablespoons flour
1 cup cold water
1/4 teaspoon grated Nutmeg
1 teaspoon salt
2 cups water
freshly grated black pepper
1/3 cup chopped fresh parsley
parmesan cheese, freshly grated

Melt butter in heavy soup pot and sauté parsnips and celery, stirring until vegetables are coated with butter. Cover and cook for 10 minutes, stirring occasionally. Heat the chicken stock in a saucepan and add to the soup pot. Stir well and put 1 cup soup (including solids) into the blender with the flour, cold water, nutmeg and salt. Blend at high speed and return to the soup pot. Add 2 cups water and simmer for 5 minutes. Season with pepper. Return another cup soup to the blender and add parsley. Blend well and return to the soup pot. Heat. When serving, sprinkle with cheese.

GARDEN CREPES

Filling:
1/4 cup butter
1/2 cup dry bread crumbs
1 tablespoon chopped fresh parsley
1/8 teaspoon pepper
2 tablespoons sherry
2 hard-cooked eggs, chopped
1 cup cooked, chopped carrots
1 cup cooked, chopped cauliflower
12 cooked crepes (see index)

Melt butter in saucepan, add breadcrumbs. Cook until light brown. Stir in parsley, pepper, wine, eggs, carrots and cauliflower. Fill cooked crepes with vegetables, fold over. Heat in 350 degree oven for 15-20 minutes. Serve with *Cheese Sauce.

*Cheese Sauce
2 tablespoons butter
2 tablespoons flour
1/4 teaspoon salt
1/8 teaspoon pepper
1 cup milk
1 cup grated cheddar cheese
1 teaspoon dry mustard
1/2 teaspoon Worcestershire sauce

Melt butter in saucepan over low heat. Blend in flour, salt and pepper. Cook over low heat, stirring until mixture is smooth and bubbly. Remove from heat. Stir in milk and heat to boiling. Add remaining ingredients, stirring constantly, until cheese is melted. Serve over hot crepes. Garnish with a sprig of summer savory and serve with a fresh half tomato stuffed with parsley.

CHICKEN PAELLA

2/3 cup butter
1 8-ounce can minced clams, drained
2/3 cup cooked chicken, cubed
1 4 1/2-ounce can small shrimp, rinsed and drained
1 4-ounce can mushroom stems and pieces, drained
1 2-ounce jar chopped pimento, drained
1/4 cup chopped fresh parsley
1/4 teaspoon garlic powder
1/4 teaspoon hot pepper sauce
1/4 cup white wine
1 teaspoon Worcestershire sauce
cooked, hot rice

In a 2 quart saucepan melt butter over medium heat. Add all the ingredients except the rice. Cook over medium heat, stirring occasionally, until heated through. Spoon over hot rice.

SOLE WITH ROQUEFORT AND SHRIMP STUFFING

1/2 cup butter, softened
3 ounces cream cheese, softened
6 ounces raw shrimp, cleaned and cut into small pieces
2 tablespoons lemon juice
1 tablespoon chopped parsley
3 ounces Roquefort cheese
1 scallion, minced
1/4 teaspoon hot pepper sauce
1/4 teaspoon Worcestershire sauce
freshly ground black pepper
10 ounces fillet of sole
2 beaten eggs
breadcrumbs

Combine all ingredients except sole, eggs and breadcrumbs in a mixing bowl. Blend thoroughly. Refrigerate filling for at least 20 minutes. Preheat oven to 375 degrees. Pat fish dry and spread about 1/4 cup chilled filling on each fillet. Roll fillet, folding in sides to hold mixture in. Dip each fillet in beaten egg and roll in breadcrumbs. Place in a buttered baking dish and top with any remaining filling. Bake for approximately 20 minutes, until sole flakes easily.

ONION CHEESE BREAD

1/2 cup onion, chopped
2 tablespoons butter
1 egg, beaten
1/2 cup milk
1 1/2 cup Bisquick
1 cup cheddar cheese, grated
2 tablespoons parsley, chopped
2 tablespoons butter, melted

Cook the onions in the butter till tender. Combine the egg and milk and add to the biscuit mix. Stir just till moistened. Add the onions, parsley and 1/2 the cheese. Spread in a greased 8" square pan. Sprinkle with the remaining cheese and drizzle with the butter. Bake at 400 degrees for 20 minutes.

MINIATURE CHEESE CAKES

1 package foil muffin baking cups
1 box vanilla wafers
3 8-ounce packages cream cheese, softened
2 eggs
1/2 cup sugar
1 can cherry pie filling

Combine cream cheese, eggs and sugar. Beat together well.
Fill muffin tins with foil baking cups and place a vanilla wafer
in the bottom of each, then add 2 teaspoons of the filling.
Bake at 350 degrees for 20 minutes. Cool to room temperature,
top each with pie filling, then cover with wax paper and chill
thoroughly.

A MENU FOR MARCH

Creamy Spinach Dip

Leek Soup

Ginger Maple Bread

Lemon Parsley Dressing for Mixed Greens

Norwegian Meat Pies

Tangy Mustard Cauliflower

Grasshopper Crepes

CREAMY SPINACH DIP

1 cup sour cream
1 cup mayonnaise
1/2 teaspoon celery salt
1/2 teaspoon dill weed
1/4 teaspoon onion powder
1/4 cup chopped scallions
1 10-ounce package frozen spinach, thawed and well drained
1 8-ounce can water chestnuts, drained and finely chopped

Combine sour cream, mayonnaise and seasonings. Stir in
scallions, spinach and water chestnuts, cover and chill. Good
served with fresh vegetables.

LEEK SOUP

1/4 cup butter
4 leeks, cleaned and sliced
1 medium onion, chopped
1/4 cup celery, thinly sliced
6 cups chicken broth
2 tablespoons chopped fresh parsley
1 tablespoon chopped fresh thyme
1/8 teaspoon ground black pepper
1 pound fresh spinach, washed and drained
1 cup half and half

Sauté the leeks, onion and celery in the butter for 10 minutes.
Place the chicken stock, sautéed vegetables, parsley, thyme and
pepper in a large saucepan. Remove thick stems from the
spinach and add the leaves to the stock. Bring to a boil, reduce
heat and simmer 20 minutes. In blender, puree the mixture in
three batches for 15 seconds each on high speed. Return to pan
and stir in the half and half. Heat until hot, but do not boil.

GINGER MAPLE BREAD

1 1/2 cups boiling water
1 cup oatmeal
1/2 cup warm water
1 teaspoon sugar
2 teaspoons ground ginger
2 packages dry yeast
4 tablespoons brown sugar
2 cups flour
2 teaspoons softened butter
2 teaspoons salt
4 tablespoons maple syrup
2 cups flour
extra flour for kneading

Pour boiling water over oatmeal in a large bowl and let stand until lukewarm. Combine with the 1/2 cup warm water, sugar, ginger and yeast and let stand until bubbly. Add brown sugar and 2 cups of flour to the oatmeal mixture. Beat well. Add butter, salt, maple syrup and 2 more cups of flour. Stir well. Knead dough until stiff on a floured board. Cover and let rise in a greased bowl until doubled in bulk. Shape into 2 loaves. Put in two greased loaf pans, cover, and let rise until doubled in bulk. Bake at 375 degrees 30 minutes or until tests done.

LEMON PARSLEY DRESSING FOR MIXED GREENS

1/4 teaspoon dried marjoram
2 teaspoons chopped green pepper
dash white pepper
1 cup chopped fresh parsley
1/2 cup oil
2 teaspoons herb vinegar
juice of 1 lemon

Place all ingredients together and blend until the parsley is fine.

NORWEGIAN MEAT PIES

1 package pie crust mix
1/4 cup brandy
1 tablespoon butter
2 onions, finely chopped
4 eggs
1 1/2 teaspoons dry mustard
3/4 teaspoon ground allspice
3/4 teaspoon ground coriander
1/2 teaspoon black pepper
1/4 teaspoon ground cloves
2 pounds lean ground pork
1 pound lean ground beef
1 1/2 cups shredded Jarlsburg cheese
1/4 cup roasted, shelled sunflower seeds
1 tablespoon cold water

Prepare pie crust mix according to package directions using
1 tablespoon brandy as part of the liquid. Divide dough in half
and refrigerate. In large skillet, cook the onions in the butter
until soft. Remove from heat, add 3 tablespoons of brandy and
cool to room temperature. In a large bowl, beat 3 eggs. Beat in

spices and the onion mixture. Add meats, cheese and seeds. Stir gently. Roll the dough into 5" circles spooning 3 tablespoons of the meat mixture onto each circle. Fold over and seal edges. Refrigerate 20 minutes. Beat remaining egg with cold water and brush the tops of each turnover. Bake at 425 degrees 20 minutes. Reduce oven temperature to 350 degrees and bake 30 minutes longer. Serve with *yogurt sauce.

*Yogurt Sauce
1 cup plain yogurt
1 cup sour cream
1 tablespoon brandy
1 teaspoon grated lemon peel
2 tablespoons snipped fresh parsley

Combine yogurt and sour cream. Stir in brandy and lemon peel until blended. Spoon into serving dish; sprinkle with parsley.

TANGY MUSTARD CAULIFLOWER

1 medium head cauliflower
1/2 cup sour cream
1 teaspoon chopped onion
1/2 teaspoon dry mustard
1/2 cup shredded cheddar

Cook cauliflower until tender. In a small bowl, combine the sour cream, onion and mustard. Spread this on the hot cauliflower and sprinkle with the cheese. Cover and let stand until the cheese melts, about 3 minutes.

GRASSHOPPER CREPES

2 cups miniature marshmallows
1/3 cup milk
2 tablespoons white Creme de Cacao
3 tablespoons green Creme de Menthe
green food color
1 cup heavy cream
*12 cooked chocolate crepes
whipped cream
1/2 ounce semi-sweet chocolate

Heat marshmallows and milk in saucepan over low heat, stirring constantly until marshmallows just melt. Refrigerate,
stirring now and then, until mixture mounds slightly when
dropped from a spoon (about 1/2 hour). Stir in Creme de
Cacao and Creme de Menthe and several drips green coloring.
Beat heavy cream until stiff. Fold green mixture into whipped
cream. Fill cooked crepes; fold over. Chill until firm. Top with
extra whipped cream. Grate chocolate or make chocolate curls
to sprinkle over crepes.

*Chocolate Crepes
3 eggs
1 cup flour
2 tablespoons sugar
2 tablespoons cocoa
1 1/4 cups buttermilk
2 tablespoons melted butter

Combine ingredients in blender for about 1 minute. Scrape
down sides with rubber spatula and blend for 15 seconds or
until smooth. Cook as for regular crepes (see index).

APRIL

Spring is come,
Tis time to plow:
The earth to till,
The seed to sow.

Many of the customs connected with Easter come from pagan festivals of spring. In most countries, Easter comes in early spring, when green grass and warm sunshine begin to push away the ice and snow of winter. The name, Easter, perhaps comes from Eostre, a Teutonic goddess of spring.

In ancient Europe, the rabbit symbolized birth and new life and was considered a symbol of the moon. Perhaps it became an Easter symbol because the moon determines the date of Easter.

As a prelude to Easter, Germans celebrate Shrove Tuesday and eat fastnachts and pretzels. In Great Britain, it is the custom to eat carling, or peas, on Carling Sunday, the fifth Sunday of Lent. Hot cross buns, with their cross-shaped topping, have ties which extend back to pre-Christian times when the cross represented both sun and fire.

Early Mesopotamian Christians were first to use colored eggs for Easter, and red dye was used to represent the joy of the Resurrection. Food is often decorated with the letters XB for *cristos voskres* (Christ is risen).

April arrives, and the frost is slowly leaving the ground. The weather teases us, and the changing temperature heaves the plants and lifts them to the elements. We hasten to tamp down their roots to protect them from still frosty nights. The bloodroot is blooming in the dye garden, and the coltsfoot will be next, with its dandelion-like flowers. We look forward to the first tender green lovage leaves – we will brew these into a spring tonic as the early countrywomen did.

We build in a natural protection for our plants by interplanting fragrant herbs, flowers, and vegetables. Strong scents confuse, thus repelling invading insects.

Tiny seedlings dropped from last year's harvest appear in unlikely spots, and tilling must wait until we have moved them to their proper homes.

Spring has put excitement into our hearts, and winter woes are forgotten.

BAY
Tender Perennial
laurus nobilis

The bay tree, since it is a tender perennial, is best kept in a large tub, where it will grow up to ten feet in height. In its native Mediterranean area, the tree grows up to sixty feet tall. Bay is a very attractive, aromatic shrub with shiny, dark green leaves.

Plant bay in a moderate soil with good drainage. On hot summer days it is best grown in filtered sun or afternoon shade. Bring the tub in during winter months. The leaves can be picked and dried year round.

Bay is not easy to propagate! Cuttings are more successful than seed, but they may take up to six months to root. I would suggest the purchase of a plant – it will amply reward you!

Do not confuse this plant with our local laurel which is poisonous and must not be used. The Greeks associated bay with prophecies, and victors and heroes were given a laurel crown. The term baccalaureate was perhaps derived from the practice – baccalaureus or laurel-berry; thus, covered with berries of laurel.

Bay was thought to provide protection against evil, and plants were often placed beside the front door. The withering of the laurel tree was once considered an omen of disaster.

The pungent bay leaves are used to drive away insects; place several leaves in canisters of flour or cereal to keep them free of pests.

Bay is a prime ingredient in bouquet garni for soups and stews. Always remove the leaf from the soup pot before serving. Bay enhances the flavor of meats, fish, and poultry, and gives a pungent aroma to marinades and casseroles. Use the leaf sparingly, for it is strong in flavor.

FISH STOCK

2-3 pounds fish bones, heads and tails
6 cups water
2 cups dry white wine
2 onions, chopped
1 leek, thinly sliced
1/4 cup fresh parsley
1 bay leaf
6 black peppercorns

Rinse the fish, crack the large bones and place all in a pot. Add the water and the wine. Boil for 5 minutes and skim off the foam. Reduce heat, add all the remaining ingredients and simmer for 30 minutes. (Skim foam as it appears.) Strain the stock and use it as a base for soups and stews.

VEGETABLE BROTH

3 onions, chopped
4 carrots, sliced
1 clove garlic
2 leeks, chopped
3 stalks celery
*Herb Bouquet

Combine all ingredients in a large soup pot and bring to a boil. Boil gently for 30-40 minutes. Strain broth and discard vegetables. Makes 1 quart. This vegetarian broth can be used as an alternative to chicken or beef broth.

*Herb Bouquet
Bay leaf
6 sprigs parsley
3 sprigs thyme
3 coriander seeds
2 whole cloves
1 sprig tarragon
1/4 teaspoon cayenne pepper

SPICY TOMATO SOUP

2 pounds soup bones
6 cups tomato juice
1 1/4 cups tomato puree
2 cups water
3 tomatoes, coarsely chopped
1 large onion stuck with 6 cloves
2 bay leaves
2 tablespoons fresh basil, chopped
2 tablespoons sugar

Place all ingredients in a large kettle and bring to a boil. Reduce heat and simmer till meat is tender. Remove bay leaves, onion and meat. Dice the meat and return it to the soup. Serve with a dollop of sour cream.

LENTIL BARLEY SOUP

2 1/4 cups raw lentils, rinsed
11 cups water
1/2 cup barley
3 bay leaves
2 cups cauliflower, chopped
2 cups broccoli, chopped
2 cups carrots, sliced
1 cup celery, sliced
1 onion, chopped
2 tablespoons fresh parsley, chopped
1 teaspoon celery seed
2 teaspoons dill weed
freshly ground black pepper
2 tablespoons vinegar

Bring the lentils and water to a boil in a large soup pot. Stir in
the barley and bay leaves and simmer for 1/2 hour, then add the
prepared vegetables. Bring to a boil, reduce heat and simmer
soup for 1 hour or until lentils are tender. Add spices and
vinegar and cook for 10 more minutes. Remove the bay leaves
before serving!

WHITE BEAN CASSEROLE

2 cups small white beans, soaked overnight
4 carrots, diced
1 red pepper, diced
1 stalk celery, diced
1 onion, sliced
3 garlic cloves, minced
1 bay leaf
1/2 teaspoon rosemary
1/2 teaspoon thyme
2 tablespoons olive oil
1 vegetable bouillon cube
10 cups water

Drain the beans and place in a heavy soup pot with water, carrots, celery, red pepper and onion. Bring to a boil and stir in the garlic, bay leaf, rosemary, thyme and oil. Simmer over low heat for 1 hour and 45 minutes. Add the bouillon cube and simmer an additional 30 minutes.

A MENU FOR APRIL

Caraway Dip

Cream of Carrot Soup

Hot Cross Buns

Tossed Salad with Spicy Dressing

Crab Strudel

Minted Peas

Jelly Roll

CARAWAY DIP

8 ounces cream cheese, softened
1 cup cottage cheese
3 tablespoons butter, softened
2 tablespoons caraway seed
1 tablespoon fresh chives, chopped fine
1/4 cup sherry
2 tablespoons light cream

Cream the cream cheese with the cottage cheese. Add the butter. Stir in the caraway seed and the chives. Blend in the sherry and cream. Serve with crackers.

CREAM OF CARROT SOUP

1 onion, diced
3 tablespoons oil
6 large carrots, thinly sliced
1 cup skim milk, powdered
3 cups water
3 cups chicken broth
1/8 teaspoon white pepper
fresh dill

Sauté onion and carrots in oil until tender. Reserve 1/3 of the carrots. Put 2/3 of the sautéed carrots in the blender and puree with the water. Combine powdered milk and broth with a whisk and add to the puree. Add pepper. Add the reserved 1/3 of the carrots to the soup and heat. Garnish with fresh dill.

HOT CROSS BUNS

2 packages yeast
1/3 cup warm water
1/3 cup scalded milk
1/2 cup butter
1/3 cup sugar
3/4 teaspoon salt
4 cups flour
1 teaspoon cinnamon
1/2 teaspoon nutmeg
1 teaspoon ground cardamon
3 well-beaten eggs
3/4 cup raisins
1/2 teaspoon lemon extract

Soften yeast in warm water. Into the scalded milk, stir the butter, sugar and salt. Let cool to lukewarm. Sift flour and spices together. Into the milk mixture stir 1 cup flour and mix well. Add eggs and extract and beat well. Add the softened yeast and the raisins. Add the remaining flour a bit at a time and mix thoroughly to make a soft dough. Cover with a damp towel and let rise 1 1/2 to 2 hours. Punch down. Roll dough 1/2" thick. Cut into rounds with a biscuit cutter and shape into 24 buns. Place well apart on a greased cookie sheet. Cover and let rise for 1 hour. With scissors, cut a cross in the center of each bun. Bake at 375 degrees for 12 minutes, or till browned. Fill cross with Frosting*.

*Frosting:
1 lightly beaten egg white
1 cup confectioner's sugar
1/2 teaspoon vanilla

Stir together until smooth and dribble a cross on each one.

SPICY DRESSING

2 teaspoons dry mustard
2 teaspoons herb salt
2 teaspoons paprika
1/4 cup sugar
1 large clove garlic, crushed
1 small onion, finely chopped
1/2 cup white wine vinegar
1 cup corn oil

Blend together well and refrigerate. Shake before serving.

CRAB STRUDEL

1 tablespoon minced scallions
4 tablespoons butter
3 tablespoons flour
1/2 teaspoon salt
1/8 teaspoon black pepper
1 1/3 cups milk
2 6-ounce packages frozen crabmeat, thawed and drained
3 tablespoons dry sherry
1/3 pound phyllo
1/4 cup breadcrumbs

Sauté scallions in a bit of butter. Stir in flour, salt and pepper and cook 1 minute. Gradually stir in the milk and cook until mixture is thickened. Add the crabmeat and sherry. Remove from heat. Melt 4 tablespoons butter. Overlap sheets of phyllo to form a 16" x 12" rectangle, brushing each layer with melted butter and sprinkling with bread crumbs. Starting at the short end, spoon crabmeat mixture on 1/2 of the rectangle and roll up. Place on cookie sheet, seam side down. Brush with remaining butter. Bake at 375 degrees for 40 minutes.

MINTED PEAS

2 pounds fresh peas
1/4 pound butter
2 tablespoons minced fresh spearmint

Cook the peas and drain. Melt the butter and add the spearmint. Add the butter mixture to the peas and serve.

JELLY ROLL

3 large eggs
1 cup sugar
5 tablespoons water
1 teaspoon vanilla
1 cup flour
1 teaspoon baking powder
1/4 teaspoon salt
confectioners sugar
soft jelly or jam

Beat the eggs till thick. Gradually beat in the sugar. Beat in the water and vanilla all at once. Sift the flour, baking powder and salt and add all at once. Beat just until smooth. Pour into a well greased jelly roll pan. Bake at 375 degrees for 12 minutes, just till cake tests done. Loosen edges and immediately turn upside down on a towel sprinkled with confectioners sugar. Spread cake at once with soft jelly or jam and roll up, beginning at short end. Wrap in a towel until cool.

ZEBROVKA

1 quart vodka
1 pinch salt
1 teaspoon sugar
1 teaspoon glycerine
6 blades zebrovka
1/2 teaspoon lemon peel

Add ingredients to vodka and store in a cool dark place for 2 weeks. Chill and drink or serve over lemon ice. A Russian Easter treat!

MAY

We've been rambling all the night
and sometime of this day
And now returning back again
We bring a garland gay.

A garland gay we bring you here
And at your door we stand
It is a sprout well budded out
The work of our Lord's hand.

Old English Ballad

May Day, the favorite festival of spring, brings us marvelous customs, costumes, decorations, dances and foods to signal the changing season.

During Medieval times, May Poles were the center of the revelry, splendid with their crowns of ribbons and streamers and decorations of flowers. Dancers with bells on their ankles and wrists stamped the ground to awaken it. May bells were rung to alert the sleeping fields and forests to the time of re-birth, and May baskets were hung on the doors.

Spring green foods were served in abundance and always included a cookie man called "Jack-in-the-bush," for on his head he wore a wreath of green.

During ancient Celtic rites, the Queen of the May directed the games of competition.

Sweet woodruff, the very essence of spring with its vibrant green leaves and early blossoms was steeped in Rhine wine to make the German Maibowle. The plant's German name – Waldmeister – means "Master of the Woods."

Traditionally, a bit of Bannock (oatmeal) cake was served and thrown to the witches, who must wait for their portion of the feast.

Sunny May mornings force us early from our beds for a trip through the gardens, and we are pleased that our spring efforts have begun to reward us with an abundance of fresh herbs for cooking. Borders of chives already need clipping and the salad burnet, with its cucumber flavor, is ready for picking.

The cats have discovered the first tender growth of the catnip and are sleeping it off in the sun-drenched wheelbarrow!

Huge pots of rosemary, sweet bay and the tender lavenders are moved outside for their summer vacation. It is time to air the drying shed, to remove the remaining remnants of last year's harvest and ready it for the new crop. Sprigs of sweet woodruff are picked for the luncheon tables and we bring out the cool-looking blue tablecloths for the summer months.

As we take a walk along the path in the woods we breathe in the earthy scents of new life.

MINT

Hardy Perennial
mentha, various species

Spearmint, *m. spicata* known as the "gourmet's mint," according to variety, can have oval, crinkly, dark green leaves or elongated, smooth bright green leaves.

Peppermint, *m. piperita officinalis*, grows to about two feet high with small pointed green leaves with a purple tint.

Orange mint, *m. piperita citrata*, has rounded green leaves that are touched with purple, as is the stem.

Egyptian mint, *m. niliaca*, grows very tall, up to five feet. The leaves are woolly grey and rounded and are often called "Fairy blankets" by English children. This variety is often confused with the smaller growing apple mint.

Corsican mint, *m. requieni*, grows only 1" high and has a mossy character, making it a beautiful ground cover for small spots.

There are dozens of mints to choose from, but most all prefer fertile soil with a high moisture holding capacity. They will grow in sun or shade and benefit from frequent cutting. Mints must be disciplined! They spread rapidly and will quickly invade a garden, overrunning other plants, so are best given a spot where they may wander at will. Seeds are slow to start and it is best to purchase plants. Varieties will cross-pollinate and must be kept separated. Mints are easily propagated by root division. The tiny Corsican mint requires shade and well-drained, moist soil. Give it some protection over the winter.

Cut mint just before coming into full flower and hang it in bunches in a dry, airy place away from sunlight. Strip the dry leaves from their stalks and store in jars.

Mint is native to Egypt and the holyland; guests in ancient Greece and Rome were seated at tables rubbed with mint leaves. From this practice comes the idea of mint as a symbol of hospitality.

Pennyroyal, a member of the mint family can be spread about and rubbed on animals to rid them of fleas.

Mints repel many garden pests such as aphids and flea beetles. Mint is also reputed to keep away mice and other rodents. Try it in lieu of poisons!

The herbalist Gerard commented: "The smell of minte does stir up the minde and the taste to a greedy desire of meate." Hang a bunch of mint in your doorway on hot summer days and the breeze will release its cooling aroma. Bowls of mint on your table will have the same cooling effect. Mints were long used as "strewing herbs" on the floors of houses and public buildings.

Spearmint and peppermint make excellent tea, served hot or cold. Any of the mints make a fragrant addition to potpourri or sleep pillows. Mint is said to aid in clearing the sinuses – as all the menthol remedies in your modern drugstore will indicate!

Spearmint is the variety most often used in julips, jellies and mint sauces. Try stuffing fresh spearmint leaves and small cloves of garlic beneath the skin of a roasting lamb before cooking it. Peppermint is a tasty addition to peas, and chopped mint is delicious with buttered potatoes, in cooling summer fruit salads and sherbets. Use mint vinegar as a tasty addition to dressings for seafood.

TABBOULI SALAD

1 cup bulghur (cracked wheat)
2 cups boiling water
2 cups parsley, finely chopped
1/2 cup scallions, chopped
1/2 cup fresh mint, chopped
1/2 cup lemon juice
1/2 cup olive oil
3 ripe tomatoes, chopped

Pour the boiling water over the wheat and let stand for one hour. Drain and return it to the bowl. Add the parsley, scallions, mint, and lemon juice. Blend well and chill. Just before serving, toss with the oil and add the chopped tomatoes.

MINT JELLY

2 tablespoons spearmint, finely chopped
1 cup apple or currant jelly

A quick and easy way to make mint jelly, simply simmer the spearmint in the jelly. Delicious as a lamb condiment!

GROUND LAMB WITH MINT

1 1/2 pounds ground lamb
1 tablespoon oil
1/2 cup onion, finely chopped
2 tablespoons fresh parsley, chopped
3 tablespoons fresh spearmint, chopped
black pepper

Combine the lamb and the pepper, Sauté the onion in the oil.
Add the onion to the lamb along with the chopped herbs. Mix
well. Form into small balls and place on a baking sheet. Bake at
350 degrees for 25 minutes, turning once. Serve with yogurt.

HERBED COTTAGE CHEESE

1 pound cottage cheese
2 tablespoons fresh chives, minced
1 teaspoon Fines Herbes
1 tablespoon Worcestershire sauce
1/4 cup fresh spearmint, minced

Mix all together and chill. Serve on a bed of greens with pineapple bits and a cherry.

CARROTS WITH MINT

2 pounds carrots
1/3 cup butter
1 tablespoon sugar
3 tablespoons chopped fresh mint

Quarter the carrots and steam until tender. Drain and return to
the pan. Add the butter and sugar. Stir over very low heat for
3 minutes. Cover and cook 2 minutes more. Add the mint and
serve.

MINT SAUCE

4 sprigs fresh spearmint
1 cup red wine vinegar
1 teaspoon sugar

Chop the mint leaves very fine. Mix the vinegar and sugar and
bring it to a boil. Pour the hot vinegar over the mint leaves,
then allow it to steep for several days.

CANDIED MINT LEAVES

1 egg
1 tablespoon orange juice
sugar
fresh, perfect leaves

Beat the egg and orange juice until frothy. Paint the leaves with this mixture, using a small paint brush. Spoon superfine sugar over the leaves, covering all sides. (You will need to keep adding dry sugar to the dish.) Lay the leaves on waxed paper and move them several times to keep them from sticking to the paper. Dry completely for several days, then store in an airtight container.

These delicate, sugar-crisp decorations make a fancy topping for cakes, ice cream and special deserts. Violets or borage blossoms may also be candied in this way.

MINT GARDEN DIP

1 cup sour cream
3 ounces cream cheese
2 tablespoons lemon juice
1 tablespoon Worcestershire sauce
3 tablespoons fresh mint, chopped
10 stuffed green olives, chopped

Mix sour cream and softened cream cheese until smooth. Add remaining ingredients and blend well. Chill.

GREEN PEA SOUP WITH MINT

2 tablespoons oil
1 onion, chopped
2 pounds frozen peas
4 1/2 cups vegetable stock
1 teaspoon thyme
freshly ground black pepper
2/3 cup half and half
2 tablespoons chopped fresh mint

Sauté the onion in the oil for 5 to 7 minutes, until soft but not browned. Add the peas and cook 2 to 3 minutes. Pour in the stock, add the thyme and bring to a boil. Simmer for 20 minutes. Puree and season with pepper. Garnish with a spoonful of sour cream and the chopped mint.

COLD GREEK LEMON SOUP

1/2 cup uncooked rice
1/2 teaspoon salt
3 quarts chicken broth
6 eggs
1/2 cup lemon juice
1 teaspoon white pepper
2 tablespoons sugar
2 lemons, sliced paper thin
fresh mint

Boil rice, salt and broth for 15 minutes. Remove from heat and set aside. Beat eggs with mixer until frothy. Beat in lemon juice, pepper and sugar. Ladle 3 cups of broth into the egg mixture, 1 cup at a time. Pour beaten egg mixture into rice mixture, stir well and refrigerate. Serve chilled, garnished with lemon slices and chopped fresh mint.

SPRING CUSTARD WITH MINT

1/3 cup cornstarch
1 quart milk
1/2 cup sugar

Cook the above ingredients over low heat until slightly thickened. Beat 2 eggs and slowly add, stirring constantly. Bring just
to a boil. Remove from stove and cool. Chill the custard thoroughly before serving with a sprig of fresh mint.

MARINATED FRUIT SAUCE

1 11-ounce can mandarin oranges
1 20-ounce can pineapple chunks
1/4 cup white Creme de Menthe
fresh mint, minced

Combine above ingredients, place in a jar and marinate overnight in the refrigerator. Turn jar upside down occasionally so
all fruit comes in contact with the liquor. Serve over lemon
sherbet or vanilla ice cream.

CHIVE BUTTER

Mash chopped chives into softened butter and allow to chill. The butter can then be cut into squares and used for later use.

The flavor of chives can be destroyed by long cooking, so add them during the last ten minutes. Chives will enhance all kinds of salads, sauces, egg dishes, and add zest to dips. Add them to baked potatoes, and sprinkle chopped chives on soup as a garnish.

FINES HERBES

For a fresh blend of fines herbes from your garden, try mixing 1/2 cup of chopped parsley, 1/4 cup chopped chives and a few chopped tarragon leaves.

CHIVE BISCUITS

2 cups flour
2 teaspoons baking powder
1/2 teaspoon herb salt
4 teaspoons butter
1/3 cup finely chopped chives
3/4 cup milk
Melted butter

Stir together the dry ingredients. Cut in the butter and add the chives. Stir in the milk with a fork. Turn out on a floured board and knead three or four times. Roll out to 1/2" thickness and cut with a biscuit cutter. Place on a buttered baking sheet and brush the tops with melted butter. Bake at 450 degrees for 12-15 minutes.

A MENU FOR MAY

Ginger Dip

Spring Garden Soup

Whole Wheat Crescent Rolls with Sesame

Shrimp and Grapefruit Salad

Asparagus Bacon Pie

Jack-in-the Bush Cookies

Maibowle (May Wine)

GINGER DIP

1 cup mayonnaise
1 cup sour cream
1/4 cup grated onion
1/4 cup minced fresh parsley
1 can water chestnuts, chopped
3 tablespoons chopped candied ginger
1 clove garlic, minced
1 tablespoon soy sauce
dash Tabasco

Combine all of the above and chill for several hours. The zippy taste of ginger in this dip will reawaken your taste buds!

SPRING GARDEN SOUP

1 large can chicken broth (skim the fat off the top)
1 can water
3 whole bay leaves
1 bag bouquet garni
jullienne vegetables

Bring all ingredients, except the vegetables, to a boil and simmer for 1 hour. Remove the bouquet garni and the 3 whole bay leaves. Pour into hot soup bowls and add a small amount of julienne vegetables. We like green peppers, onion, carrots and scallions; all must be sliced paper thin.

WHOLE WHEAT CRESCENT ROLLS WITH SESAME

4 teaspoons dry yeast
1 cup lukewarm water
1 teaspoon honey
1 cup oil
3 tablespoons honey
2 teaspoons salt
1 cup boiling water
2 eggs, beaten
6 cups whole wheat flour
1 egg, beaten
1/2 teaspoon water
1/2 cup sesame seeds (toasted for 20 minutes in a 200 degree oven)

Dissolve yeast in lukewarm water. Add 1 teaspoon honey. In large bowl mix oil, 3 tablespoons honey, salt and boiling water. When lukewarm, add 2 beaten eggs, then dissolved yeast. Gradually stir in whole wheat flour, mix well but do not knead. Chill until firm. Divide dough in 3 parts and roll each into a large circle, as thin as possible. Brush with beaten egg to which 1/2 teaspoon water has been added. Sprinkle sesame seeds over the surface. Cut each circle into wedges about 2 inches wide at the outside edge. Roll each edge toward the center, lift up and dip in egg mixture, then in sesame seeds. Place on oiled cookie sheets, leaving room to rise. Let rise 1 1/2 hours. Bake at 425 degrees for 15 minutes or more until golden brown.

SHRIMP AND GRAPEFRUIT SALAD

1 cup shrimp
2 cups grapefruit segments, chilled
3 ounces cream cheese, softened
2 tablespoons mayonnaise
5-6 pieces crisp celery
French dressing

Clean the cooked shrimp and cup into small pieces. Drain grapefruit. Mash the cream cheese, add the mayonnaise and mix well together. Add the shrimp and mix well. Pack grooves of celery tightly with this mixture. Cut into 3/4" slices. Arrange on crisp lettuce leaves with grapefruit segments. Sprinkle with French dressing. Garnish with a sprig of tarragon.

ASPARAGUS BACON PIE

3 cups cooked asparagus cut in 1-inch pieces
6 slices crisp cooked bacon
3 eggs lightly beaten
1 tablespoon chopped scallions
1 teaspoon sugar
1/4 teaspoon pepper
pinch nutmeg
1/2 cup cream
1 cup grated parmesan cheese
pastry for 9" pie shell

Line a pie plate with the pastry. Spread the crumbled bacon on the bottom. Arrange the asparagus over the bacon. Mix together the eggs, scallions, sugar, pepper, nutmeg, cream and half the cheese. Pour over the asparagus. Spread the remaining cheese on top and bake for 10 minutes at 400 degrees. Reduce oven heat to 350 degrees and bake for 25-30 minutes longer.

JACK-IN-THE-BUSH COOKIES

1 1/2 cups soft butter or margarine
2 cups sugar
4 eggs
2 teaspoons vanilla
5 cups flour
2 teaspoons baking powder
2 teaspoons salt

Mix together the sugar, eggs and vanilla. Blend in the flour, baking powder, salt. Chill 1 hour. Heat oven to 400 degrees. Roll the dough 1/8" thick on lightly floured board. Cut with a gingerbread boy cutter and place on ungreased baking sheet. Sprinkle a wreath of green sugar sprinkles on each boy's head. Bake about 6-8 minutes or until very light brown.

MAIBOWLE (MAY WINE)

1 small bunch sweet woodruff
1 bottle moselle or rhine wine
2 tablespoons sugar
2/3 cup water
1 pint fresh strawberries

Remove damaged leaves from the woodruff and put the whole bunch, including flowers into a tall glass jug. Pour over the wine. Gently heat the sugar and water in a pan and add to the wine. Cover loosely and chill. When serving, add fresh strawberry slices.

JUNE

On the vigil of St. John the Baptist, every man's door is shadowed with green birch, long fennel, St. John's Wort, Orphen, White Lilies and such like.

from *Everyman in His Humor*

In the old Latin calendar, June was the fourth month and had 29 days. Its name originally denoted the month in which crops grew to ripeness.

Midsummer Eve was a merry time of mixing customs of ancient sun worship with Medieval Christian lore.

Cuckoo-foot ale was a highlight of the Midsummer feast. It was spiced with ginger, anise and basil, and celebrated the cuckoo bird, who's song is a sure proof of the summer season.

In the 16th century, it was the custom for nearly every village in Germany to have a bonfire on the eve of St. John, June 23rd. Perhaps the ancient peoples built their fires to hold the warmth in the heavens as the summer solstice approached.

St. John's Eve was also the time when the magic fernseed was gathered to render one invisible, and crowns of mugwort were worn.

St. John's Wort, the Baptist's particular flower, was blessed and hung upon doors and windows as protection against thunder and evil spirits.

Mugwort is another plant of St. John, who wore a wreath of it in the wilderness for protection. As in the early days, leaves of mugwort are gathered on St. John's Eve and made into a cross which is placed on our roof for protection from "evil spirits!"

"Tis June, the month of roses," and the sweet scent of our old-fashioned cabbage roses is in the air. They are lovely in full bloom, but we must force ourselves to snip some in bud form to dry and fashion into our rosebud wreaths. Rose petals are picked in the early morning when the dew has dried and the blossom is at the peak of its bloom. These we dry on screens upstairs in the barn, away from the breeze.

June is the best time to visit us for a garden tour. The culinary garden is closest to the kitchen door and the various thymes intermingle with the pungent sage and winter savory. Here you will find the herbs we brew into refreshing teas – bergamot, feverfew and camomile, hyssop and horehound.

Wander into the silver garden, beautiful with its grey-green and silvery foliage. By far the favorite in this garden is the lamb's ear, as soft and woolly as its name belies. Look for the silver thyme, and the rich carpet of snow-in-summer; and in the center of the garden, an English lavender, its foliage equally as fragrant as its spikes of flowers.

Beyond the pear tree you will find the Dye Garden. Bricks form the outside circle of this garden and in each "spoke" grows a different herb that can be used to dye fabrics: dyer's camomile, laden with bright yellow daisy-like blooms, weld and woad and agrimony – strange names indeed! Here lies ladies bedstraw, once used to stuff mattresses and to curdle milk for puddings and in the center of the garden we find teasel, prickly enough to be used for carding wool!

It seems we have waited all year for this favorite month and we bask in its warmth!

LOVAGE

Hardy Perennial
levisticum officinale

Lovage is a tall plant, reaching six feet in ideal conditions. The leaves resemble celery in appearance, odor and taste. The flowers are yellow and are followed by oblong brown seeds.

Fresh seed may be sown in the ground, preferably in early fall. Plants should be divided as they get older to keep them growing vigorously. Lovage prefers partial shade with soil that is deep and fertile. Heavy fertilization and manure and lime will enhance the plant. Lovage likes a moist soil, but it must have proper drainage. It will require watering in dry weather. Usually one lovage plant is sufficient for the average family.

The lovage plant turns yellow in late summer. Cut the small leaflets off the stems before they begin to turn color and dry them on screens until very crisp. Store the dry leaves in a tight container away from light. Lovage does not store well for longer than one year.

Country women often used lovage tea as a simple remedy for aches and pains. During the middle ages, lovage was added to love potions to ensure everlasting devotion! The versatile lovage can be used in salads, soups, casseroles, cheese dishes, sauces or herb butter. The seeds of the lovage plant can be eaten with meats or in salads. In England, the seeds are candied and eaten as a confection.

Lovage is considered a deodorising herb. Try steeping fresh leaves in the bath water for an overall body freshener.

SCALLOPED POTATOES WITH LOVAGE

2 tablespoons butter
1 tablespoon flour
1 1/2 cups milk
4 potatoes, peeled and sliced
1/2 cup sharp cheddar cheese, grated
1 tablespoon fresh lovage, chopped
1 onion, chopped fine

Melt the butter and stir in the flour. Add the milk slowly,
stirring constantly. Cook and stir over low heat until thickened.
Add the lovage. In a buttered baking dish, layer the potatoes
and the onion. Pour the sauce over the top and sprinkle with
grated cheese. Bake at 350 degrees about 1 1/4 hours or until
tender.

CREAM OF LOVAGE SOUP

1 clove garlic, minced
1 1/2 cups onions, sliced
3 tablespoons butter
1/4 cup flour
5 cups chicken broth
1 1/3 cups half and half
3 tablespoons chopped fresh lovage leaves
5 cups potatoes, peeled and sliced
freshly ground black pepper

Sauté the garlic and onions in the butter until soft. Remove
from heat and stir in the flour. Slowly stir in the chicken broth.
Return to heat and bring to a boil, stirring constantly. Add the
lovage, potatoes and pepper and simmer for 30 minutes until
the potatoes are tender. Stir in the half and half and heat. Puree
the soup in the blender in small batches. Heat gently and serve.

LOVAGE SAUCE FOR FISH

2 tablespoons butter
1/4 cup lovage leaves, chopped
2 tablespoons flour
pepper to taste
1 cup milk

Sauté the lovage in the butter. Stir in the flour and pepper.
Gradually stir in the milk. Cook, stirring, until the sauce is
thickened. Serve over fish.

SUMMER SALAD

4 ripe tomatoes, quartered
1 red onion, sliced
1 green pepper, chopped
1 tablespoon wine vinegar
2 tablespoons fresh lovage, chopped
freshly ground black pepper
1/4 cup olive oil

Toss together all the ingredients and chill for several hours.
Serve on a bed of garden lettuce.

IRISH BEEF STEW WITH LOVAGE

1 1/2 pounds stewing beef, cut in small chunks
4 potatoes, peeled and diced
1 large onion, chopped
2 stalks celery, diced
6 carrots, diced
1/2 package onion and mushroom soup mix (dry)
1 can golden mushroom soup
1 can water
2 tablespoons dried lovage leaves

Combine all in a large casserole dish and bake, covered, at 325 degrees for 2 1/2 to 3 hours.

LOVAGE DIP

3 hard boiled eggs,
1/2 cup fresh lovage leaves, chopped
1/4 cup of minced parsley
sprig of minced tarragon
1 cup cottage cheese
1 cup sour cream
pepper to taste

Chill the eggs, then chop them very fine. Combine with lovage, parsley and tarragon. Add cottage cheese to the mixture and mix well. Add sour cream and pepper to taste. Chill to blend flavors.

CRABMEAT QUICHE

1 9-inch pie shell, unbaked
1 1/2 cups crabmeat
4 eggs, lightly beaten
2 cups light cream
1 teaspoon herb salt substitute
1/2 teaspoon nutmeg
dash pepper
2 tablespoons chopped lovage leaves
2 tablespoons chopped parsley
1 tablespoon chopped onion
2 tablespoons dry sherry

Beat the eggs and use a bit to brush the pie shell. Chill shell while preparing the filling. Remove all bits of cartilage and shell from the crabmeat and break it into coarse chunks. Combine the lovage, parsley, onion and sherry with the crabmeat and spread in the pie shell. Mix together the eggs, cream and seasoning. Pour the egg mixture over. Bake at 425 degrees for 35 minutes. Reduce heat to 375 degrees and cook 15 minutes more or until a knife inserted in the pie comes out clean. Garnish with a fresh sprig of lemon thyme.

GREEK LENTIL SOUP

2 cups uncooked lentils
6 cups chicken stock
2 cups water
1/2 onion, chopped
1 carrot, chopped
1/4 cup fresh lovage leaves, chopped
1 small potato, chopped
2 bay leaves
2 teaspoons vinegar

Mix all the ingredients, except the vinegar, and cook until the lentils are very soft, about one hour. Add the vinegar just before serving.

TOP ONION DIP

1 8-ounce package cream cheese, softened
12 ounces plain yogurt
2/3 cup mayonnaise
3 tablespoons parsley, chopped
6 Egyptian onions with some of the green stalks, chopped
2 teaspoons dill weed
2 teaspoons celery seed

Blend together the yogurt and cream cheese. Whip in the mayonnaise. Add the remaining ingredients and chill. Serve with fresh vegetables.

CREAMY GARLIC HERB CHEESE

2 8-ounce packages cream cheese, softened
1 pint sour cream
1/2 cup butter, softened
3 cloves garlic, crushed
1/4 cup snipped chives

Mix all ingredients in a food processor. Chill for several hours. Soften at room temperature before serving with fresh raw vegetables.

A MENU FOR JUNE

Curry Cheese Spread

Wedding Soup

Glazed Lemon Bread

Spinach Salad with Creamy Lemon Dressing

Chicken in a Blanket

Saffron Rice

Strawberry Crepes

CURRY CHEESE SPREAD

8 ounces cream cheese, softened
1 cup sharp cheddar cheese, grated
1/4 cup dry white wine
1 teaspoon curry powder
1 tablespoon grated onion

Blend well the cream cheese and the sharp cheese. Stir in the remaining ingredients. Serve with crackers.

WEDDING SOUP

6 cups chicken broth
3 tablespoons butter
1 pound lean ground lamb
2 tablespoons flour
1 onion, cut in half
cinnamon
freshly ground black pepper
2 teaspoons paprika
4 egg yolks, lightly beaten with 1 tablespoon lemon juice
1 cup plain yogurt (room temperature)

Heat the chicken broth to boiling. Heat the butter in a frying pan and fry the lamb until lightly browned. Stir in the flour and cook for 2 minutes, then transfer to the chicken broth. Add the onion, pepper and paprika to the hot broth. Reduce the heat and simmer for 1 1/2 hours. Discard the onion. Beat the egg yolks and lemon juice together. Stir in the yogurt. Add the mixture to the soup, stirring constantly until the yogurt is hot. Do not let the soup regain boiling point or the egg yolks will scramble. Serve and sprinkle with cinnamon. This is a very old recipe from Turkey that contains lamb, egg yolks, and yogurt, which are traditional ingredients to insure a fertile marriage!

GLAZED LEMON BREAD

1 cup sugar
6 tablespoons melted butter
1 teaspoon salt
rind of 1 lemon, grated
2 eggs
1/2 cup milk
1 1/2 cups flour
1 teaspoon baking powder
1/2 cup pecans, chopped

Cream sugar and shortening, add salt, lemon rind and eggs, one at a time, beating after each. Mix the flour and baking powder and add alternately with the milk. Fold in the nuts. Bake in a greased loaf pan at 350 degrees for 1 hour or more. While bread is still hot in the pan, spoon over the loaf a mixture of the juice of 1 lemon and 1/3 cup sugar. Let the bread cool in the pan.

SPINACH SALAD WITH CREAMY LEMON DRESSING

1/2 cup sour cream
1 tablespoon olive oil
3 tablespoons lemon juice
1/2 teaspoon ground ginger
salt, pepper and sugar to taste

In a small mixing bowl, combine the ingredients. Serve over a salad of fresh spinach, sliced mushrooms and sprouts.

CHICKEN IN A BLANKET

1 3-ounce package cream cheese, softened
2 tablespoons butter
2 cups cooked chicken, cubed
2 tablespoons milk
2 tablespoons fresh chives, chopped
2 tablespoons scallions, chopped
2 tablespoons pimento, minced
1 package crescent rolls
1 can cream of mushroom soup
1 cup sour cream
1/4 cup milk
1/4 pound fresh mushrooms, sliced and sautéed

Blend the cream cheese and butter. Add the chicken, 2 table-spoons milk, chives, scallions, and pimento and mix well. Combine 2 rolls to form a rectangle. Place 2 tablespoons filling on each rectangle. Bring the ends together to form a square and pinch to seal ends. Bake at 350 degrees for 20 minutes. To make the sauce, combine the cream of mushroom soup, sour cream, 1/4 cup milk and fresh mushrooms, heat and serve over the baked chicken.

SAFFRON RICE

1 cup uncooked Basmati Rice
1 teaspoon Mexican saffron
2 cups boiling water
3 tablespoons butter
1 teaspoon ground cinnamon
pinch ground cloves
1/2 cup chopped onions
1/2 teaspoon salt
1/8 teaspoon ground cardamon

Wash rice until clear. Place saffron in enough boiling water to cover and soak for 10 minutes. Heat the butter and add the cinnamon, cloves and onions. Sauté until the onions are tender, stirring constantly. Add the rice to the onions and blend, then add the boiling water, plus the saffron water. (Strain and squeeze the saffron.) Add the salt and cardamon. Stir, reduce heat to low. Cover and cook until all water is absorbed, about 20-25 minutes.

STRAWBERRY CREPES

10-12 cooked crepes (see index)
3 cups fresh strawberries
1/3 cup sugar
1 cup cottage cheese
1 cup sour cream
1/2 cup confectioner's sugar
whipped cream

Slice the strawberries, add the sugar and set aside. In the blender, whip the cottage cheese until smooth. Stir in the sour cream and the confectioner's sugar. Fill the crepes with berries and then the cheese mixture and fold over. Top with more berries and whipped cream. Add a fresh green lemon balm leaf to each crepe.

JULY

A swarm of bees in May is worth a
load of hay.
A swarm of bees in June is worth
a silver spoon.
A swarm of bees in July is not
worth a fly.

The month of July celebrates summer's abundance of fruits, vegetables and herbs. Celebrated in England is St. Swithin's Day, July 15. Rain on St. Swithin's Day is said to predict rain for forty days. A dry St. Swithin's Day means forty days of drought. Apples watered by a St. Swithin's Day rain become the most delicious.

July, the seventh month in our calendar, was originally the fifth month of the year. The name Julius (July) was given in honor of Julius Caesar who was born in this month. Anglo Saxons called July "Mead Month" because the meadows were in full bloom.

Medieval scientists took sun and star measurements on St. Swithin's Day to design almanacs for the coming year. These guides helped determine the proper time for planting, harvesting and traveling.

It is July, and we are on our knees daily to keep ahead of the weeds! We are happy to have great bunches of fresh flowers for the dining room: golden marguerite and yellow day lilies, deep blue hyssop and the brilliant red bee balm.

The harvesting of many wild flowers for drying has begun; as many as 300 bunches a day must be bundled with an elastic and hung from the rafters in the barn. Already we are picking purple lustrife, white yarrow and hops clover. Soon St. John's Wort will be added to the list. The mint is ready for its first haircut; we find it benefits from frequent cutting and sometimes harvest it three times during the summer.

We watch the roadsides for pearly everlasting and pick it early, just as the blossoms are forming. Fields of yellow goldenrod beckon to us!

For a tasty summertime snack, we stuff long stalks of the Egyptian Onion with cream cheese and stir tall glasses of cold spice tea with long cinnamon sticks.

July offers us a fine variety of fragrant blossoms for making little bouquets called "tussie mussles." Each flower has a special meaning and conveys a message to the recipient! We select rosemary for remembrance, sage for immortality, thyme for bravery, borage for courage and lavender for good wishes.

The bees are busy in the thyme, and the hummingbirds are stealing sweet nectar from the trumpet vine. We enjoy a late evening walk, armed with pennyroyal to ward off the mosquitoes!

Gallon jugs stand in stately rows filled with a variety of herb vinegars. Opal basil, tarragon, mint, and a blend of seven herbs are our favorites.

The garden offers a myriad of flowers for enhancing succulent dishes from the kitchen – nasturtiums, heart's ease, borage flowers and calendula petals greet surprised luncheon guests!

July is a busy time, for we are eager to garner all the benefits we can from Mother Earth.

TARRAGON, FRENCH

Hardy Perennial
artemisia dracunculus

In a proper location, tarragon will grow up to three feet. The upright green stems carry elongated dark green leaves. Beware when buying tarragon, and always look for the French variety. The Russian tarragon is but a poor substitute, lacking in flavor.

French tarragon never sets seed, so a plant must be purchased. Allow 15" between plants. Tarragon likes a well drained soil and lots of sun. The plant dies back to the ground during the winter and should be mulched in cold climates. Tarragon has a sharp, biting flavor with a hint of licorice. Root division may be done in early spring, and cuttings may be taken after the plant begins to show new growth in early spring.

Harvest tarragon in mid-summer, leaving two or three inches of stem. Strip the leaves from the stem and dry them carefully on screens in a dry, airy spot. Seal in a dry container.

The name tarragon is derived from the French word *estragon*, meaning "little dragon." It was recorded that tarragon cured the bites of venomous insects and mad dogs! During the Middle Ages, tarragon was thought to improve stamina, and sprigs of it were tucked into the shoes of journeyers.

Tarragon is a necessary ingredient in a blend of *fines herbes*, and imparts a delicious flavor to vinegars. Use it with poultry, fish, egg dishes, mayonnaise or butters.

Don't use this herb with a heavy hand since it can be dominating and overshadow other flavors. Avoid bringing out its bitter side by over cooking.

Tarragon leaves can be used fresh in salads, as garnishes, or in tarter sauce, bernaise sauce or French dressing.

Tarragon is an excellent windowsill plant for a sunny window. Be sure that the roots get good drainage.

POTATOES WITH TARRAGON

Cook new potatoes in their jackets until tender. Warm sour cream slightly, mix in fresh chopped tarragon and serve over the potatoes.

BROILED TOMATOES

1/2 cup dry breadcrumbs, crushed
3 tablespoons fines herbes
4 or 5 ripe tomatoes, sliced 1/4" thick
2 tablespoons grated parmesan cheese
2 tablespoons butter

Combine the crushed breadcrumbs and the herbs. Cover each tomato with the crumb mixture, then roll them in the grated cheese. Place on a buttered sheet and add a dot of butter to each tomato slice. Broil for 10 minutes.

BERNAISE SAUCE

1/4 cup tarragon vinegar
1/4 cup onion, finely chopped
1 tablespoon fresh tarragon, minced
1 teaspoon fresh parsley, minced
2 large egg yolks
8 tablespoons unsalted butter

In a small saucepan, combine the vinegar, onion and herbs.
Simmer over very low heat until only 1 tablespoon is left. Strain
into a double boiler and add the egg yolks, mixing thoroughly.
Add the butter, 2 tablespoons at a time, beating each time until
the butter is melted and mixed with the eggs. The sauce will
thicken as it cools. A delicious sauce for steak or chicken.

To make your own blend of fines herbes, combine 1 tablespoon
each of tarragon, chervil, summer savory, basil and chives.

TARRAGON BUTTER SAUCE

1/2 cup butter
1 tablespoon lemon juice
2 teaspoons tarragon, chopped

Melt the butter over low heat and stir in the lemon juice and
herb. Serve with fish or shellfish.

ZUCCHINI WITH HERBS

2 pounds zucchini
4 tablespoons olive oil
2 tablespoons butter
3 cloves garlic, crushed
1 tablespoon chopped fresh chives
2 tablespoons chopped fresh tarragon
2 tablespoons chopped fresh parsley

Cut the zucchini into 1/8" slices. Cook in a skillet in the hot oil for about 6 minutes. Drain the zucchini. Add the butter to the skillet and add the cooked zucchini. Add the garlic and herbs and mix well. Serve hot.

ONION TARRAGON PIE

pastry to line a 9" pie pan
1 cup onion, finely sliced
2 tablespoons butter
3/4 cup cheddar cheese, grated
3 eggs, slightly beaten
1 1/2 tablespoons flour
1/2 cup milk
2 teaspoons prepared mustard
2 tablespoons fresh tarragon, chopped
1 can golden mushroom soup

Sauté the onions in the butter. Line the pie pan with the pastry and place the onions on the pie shell. Sprinkle with the grated cheese. Blend together the eggs, flour, milk, mustard, tarragon and soup and pour over the onions and cheese. Bake at 350 degrees for 45 minutes or until set.

HAM OMELET WITH TARRAGON

6 eggs, separated
1/2 cup sour cream
1 cup cooked ham, chopped
2 tablespoons fresh tarragon, chopped
2 tablespoons butter

Preheat oven to 325 degrees. In a large mixing bowl, beat the egg whites until stiff. In a small bowl, beat the egg yolks until light colored, then beat in the sour cream. Pour this over the egg whites and fold in the ham and tarragon. Blend together. Melt the butter in a 10" ovenproof skillet. Pour in the omelet mixture and cook over low heat for five minutes. Transfer the skillet to the oven and bake until set, about 12 minutes. Loosen edges and invert onto a warm, buttered serving plate.

CARROTS IN TARRAGON BUTTER

4 cups sliced carrots
2 tablespoons water
3 tablespoons butter
1 tablespoon fresh tarragon, chopped
1 tablespoon fresh parsley, chopped

Cook the carrots, covered, in the water and butter until tender, about 15 minutes. Stir in the herbs and serve.

CHICKEN TARRAGON

5 chicken breasts, boned
2 cups sour cream
2 tablespoons lemon juice
4 tablespoons fresh tarragon, chopped
1 teaspoon onion, chopped
2 teaspoons paprika
1/4 pound butter
Herb Bread Crumbs (See index)

Mix the sour cream, lemon juice, tarragon, onion, and paprika in a large bowl. Place the chicken in the marinade and turn to coat all sides. Refrigerate overnight. Remove the chicken and roll in the bread crumbs. Melt the butter in a large baking pan, then add the chicken, pouring extra marinade over. Bake at 350 degrees for 1 hour.

HERB CHEESE DRESSING

2 cups olive oil
1 2-ounce can of anchovies with oil
1 3-ounce wedge blue cheese
1 teaspoon salad herbs
1 teaspoon paprika
1/2 teaspoon black pepper
1/4 cup tarragon vinegar

Whip everything together in the blender. Store in the refrigerator.

BASIC CREPES

2 fresh eggs at room temperature
1 cup milk
1 cup flour
1 tablespoon melted butter

In blender mix together the eggs and milk for 30 seconds.
Keeping speed on low, slowly add the flour and butter, just
until blended. Grease lightly a 7" skillet. Pour a scant 1/4 cup
of batter on the pan. Tilt the pan so batter spreads evenly.
Brown the bottom of the crepe lightly and remove from the
pan when the top becomes dry.

HAM ASPARAGUS CREPE

4 crepes (see index)
4 slices lean ham
8 spears asparagus, cooked
*Tarragon Hollandaise Sauce

Place one slice of lean ham on the unbrowned side of the crepe.
Place 2 spears of cooked asparagus, end to end, on the ham.
Roll to form a cigar shaped crepe. Tips of asparagus should
show outside the crepe. Warm at 300 degrees for 15 minutes.
Serve with *Tarragon Hollandaise Sauce.

*Tarragon Hollandaise Sauce
1/2 cup butter
2 egg yolks, well beaten
1 tablespoon lemon juice
1 teaspoon dried tarragon

Divide the butter into 3 portions. Put egg yolks and 1/3 of the butter into top of a double boiler over hot water. Beat constantly with a wire whisk. When butter melts, add another portion. As the mixture thickens add the remaining 1/3 butter. Remove from heat and add the lemon juice and tarragon. Serve immediately.

SHAKER HERB SOUP

4 tablespoons butter
1 cup finely chopped celery
3 tablespoons finely cut fresh chives
1 tablespoon crumbled dried chervil
1 teaspoon crumbled dried tarragon
1 quart chicken stock
freshly ground pepper
freshly grated nutmeg
1 cup grated cheddar cheese

In a heavy 2 quart saucepan, melt the butter over medium heat. Add the celery and chives and cook for 5 minutes, stirring frequently, until they are soft but not brown. Stir in the chervil and tarragon and cook for 1 minute. Add the chicken stock and a few grindings of pepper and bring the soup to a boil. Reduce heat and simmer for 20 minutes. Ladle into heated bowls and sprinkle with a bit of nutmeg. Serve at once, accompanied by a bowl of grated cheese.

CURRY DIP

1 cup mayonnaise
1 teaspoon dried tarragon
1 teaspoon garlic powder
1 teaspoon minced onion
1 teaspoon curry powder

Mix all the ingredients and chill overnight. Serve with raw vegetables.

MUSHROOM SOUP WITH SHERRY

1 1/2 pounds fresh mushrooms
2 tablespoons unsalted butter
3 tablespoons minced shallots
1/2 teaspoon salt
1 cup heavy cream (room temperature)
1/2 cup dry sherry
1 tablespoon finely snipped fresh tarragon or 1/2 teaspoon dried tarragon
3 cups yogurt (room temperature)
1/4 teaspoon white pepper

Trim and chop the mushrooms very fine. In a 2 quart saucepan melt the butter over medium-low heat and sauté the shallots until they are wilted. Add the chopped mushrooms, salt and pepper. Stir and continue sautéing until the mixture begins to dry (about 20 minutes). Add the sherry and tarragon. Simmer over medium heat until the sherry is reduced to 1/4 cup. Lower the heat and whisk in the yogurt. Simmer for 15 minutes, then add the cream. Garnish with fresh tarragon.

FRUIT SALAD

On a bed of lettuce arrange grapes, slices of banana, orange and apple, and top with a maraschino cherry. Serve with *French Dressing with Tarragon.

*French Dressing with Tarragon
1/2 cup vegetable oil
2 teaspoons lemon juice
2 tablespoons tarragon vinegar
1/4 teaspoon mustard powder
1/4 teaspoon paprika
dash freshly ground pepper
1/4 teaspoon dried tarragon

Blend all together and shake well. Garnish with a fresh sprig of tarragon.

A MENU FOR JULY

Celery Seed Dip

Gazpacho (Spanish Soup)

Cheddar Chive Crisps

Herb Dressing over Fresh Summer Greens

Lasagna Roll-ups

Blueberry Swirl Pie

CELERY SEED DIP

1 cup sour cream
2 tablespoons tarragon vinegar
1/4 teaspoon white pepper
2 teaspoons celery seeds

Combine all and chill.

GAZPACHO (SPANISH SOUP)

1 medium cucumber, cubed
4 fresh tomatoes, quartered
1 small onion, quartered
1 large green pepper, quartered
1 tablespoon sugar
1 slice bread soaked in red wine
1/2 cup water
1 egg, hard cooked
5 tablespoons wine vinegar
9 tablespoons olive oil
pepper to taste

Put everything into the blender, item by item, allowing
30 seconds per item. Blend one more minute. If too thick
add ice cubes. Chill and serve with croutons.

CHEDDAR CHIVE CRISPS

1/2 pound (2 cups) shredded cheddar cheese
2 tablespoons finely chopped fresh chives
1 1/2 cups flour
dash of cayenne
1/2 cup soft butter or margarine
1/2 teaspoon salt

Combine the cheese, butter, salt, cayenne and chives. Add the
flour. Divide the dough in half and shape each into a log about
1 1/2" in diameter. Wrap in wax paper and chill. Slice into
1/8" slices and bake on a lightly greased sheet at 350 degrees
for 10 minutes or until lightly browned. Makes about 4 dozen.

HERB DRESSING OVER FRESH SUMMER GREENS

1/4 cup tarragon vinegar
2 tablespoons sugar
1 tablespoon dill weed
1/4 teaspoon white pepper
1 1/2 cups mayonnaise
milk

Combine all in the blender. Add enough milk (about
2 or 3 tablespoons) to make the dressing easy to pour.
Serve over a salad composed of:

crisp lettuce
grated carrots
celery, cut fine
red onions
tomatoes
calendula petals (for garnish)

LASAGNA ROLL-UPS

3/4 pound lasagna cooked al dente

Filling:
1 cup ricotta cheese
1 egg yolk
1/2 teaspoon nutmeg
2 drops hot pepper sauce
pepper to taste
1/2 cup mozzarella, grated
1/3 cup grated parmesan
1/4 cup ground walnuts

Combine all ingredients in a bowl and stir well. Spread 1 to 2 tablespoons filling over each noodle and roll up end to end. Cut each roll up in half. Place cut side down in a greased baking dish. Spoon 1 to 2 teaspoons pesto sauce over each roll-up. Cover tightly with buttered foil and bake at 300 degrees for 20 minutes.

BLUEBERRY SWIRL PIE

1/2 cup butter or margarine
3/4 cup flour
1/2 cup rolled oats
1/2 cup chopped nuts
2 tablespoons sugar

Filling:
1 package lemon gelatin
1/2 cup sour cream with 1/4 teaspoon cinnamon added
2 1/4 cups prepared blueberry pie filling
1/2 cup boiling water

In saucepan melt butter. Stir in next four ingredients. Mix well and pat into 9" pie pan. Bake at 400 degrees for 12-15 minutes until golden brown. Cool. Dissolve gelatin in boiling water. Stir in blueberry filling. Chill until thickened. Pour into pie crust. Spoon sour cream onto filling by tablespoons. Cut through sour cream and lightly fold filling over it, making swirls. Chill.

AUGUST

Harvest the wheat
flail the grain
that all the earth
may bake bread again.

August is called "High Summer" or "Hohsum" and celebrates the fulfillment of the growing season. This is the time of Lammastide, when the first loaves of bread baked from the new crop of wheat were consecrated. Gates of the harvest fields were opened and sheep and other animals were allowed to graze on these "Lammas Fields." Every townhouse, country cottage and noble castle shared a Lammas feast.

The spirit of the wheat was preserved in the corn dolly, made from the last sheaf of corn. The ancient craft of corn dolly making goes back thousands of years when it was thought that a spirit lived in the cornfield which died when the corn (wheat) was cut. To preserve this spirit and insure the success of next year's harvest, a corn idol was made for the spirit to rest in. The corn dolly has become a decorative symbol of peace and prosperity in the home throughout the year.

The hot, lazy days of August, often called "dog days," wear us to a frazzle. Our Irish Setter, Duncan, has dug a hole in the damp ground under the lilac tree, hoping for a cool spot in which to rest. We pray for a cooling shower or even a thunderstorm to clear the air, and have faith that our mugwort cross on the roof will protect us from lightening! An icy glass of lemon balm tea is a welcome respite.

The goldenrod is ripening, and we wade into the swamps to collect great bunches of joe pye weed. We have decorated the dining room with a collection of corn dollies and bunches of wheat to celebrate the Lammastide. Fruit is ripening on the pear tree, and we check to see if the elderberries are ready to be made into jelly. If so, we will have purple fingers for a day or two! A mourning dove has taken up residence nearby and we hear his mournful sigh in the early evening hours.

The growing season has begun to wind down, and the days are getting shorter. Hopefully it has been a fruitful season, and we relax a bit and are happy with the fruits of our labors.

SWEET BASIL

Annual
ocimum basilicum

Basil is a medium-sized plant growing to two feet in height, and when in blossom has white or purplish flowers.

Dark opal basil has reddish-purple foliage and is striking against the greens and greys of the herb garden.

Bush basil, a compact variety, is suitable for growing in pots on a terrace, but not as an indoor plant.

Basil gives off a very pungent odor and a clove-like flavor. It likes a rich moist soil and grows in sun to partial shade. Sow the seed in the ground, or if started indoors, transplant the young shoots to the garden after all danger of frost is past, keeping them 12" apart.

Basil and rue are enemies, and do not grow well near each other. Harvest basil before it goes to flower. For the first cutting, take the main stem, leaving several shoots intact on the lower stem. These shoots will be ready for another cutting in two or three weeks. Cut off all the flower buds to keep the plant producing. The first frost will kill basil, so you will want to freeze some in ice cubes for winter use. If basil is to be dried, pinch the leaves off at the stem and dry them on screens. If after three days the leaves have not dried, continue the process in a low oven.

In various parts of Italy, basil is called "Kiss-Me-Nicholas" and is considered a token of love. A pot of basil on a balcony is a sign that the girl within will receive her suitor!

An old book refers to the powers of basil for chasing away flies; hang a bunch in your kitchen doorway and enjoy its fragrant bouquet.

Basil is known as the "tomato herb" since it has a special affinity with tomato dishes. It is even said to aid the growth of tomatoes when planted near them in the garden. It is excellent with eggplant and summer squash, and of course use lots of it in the summer salad bowl. Try replacing lettuce with basil in a sandwich. Basil is traditional in such Italian favorites as lasagna, spaghetti and pizza.

The fresh leaves of basil can be boiled and eaten as a vegetable dish. Basil makes a savory vinegar, and opal basil will give it a marvelous deep purple color.

When making garlic bread, add some finely chopped, fresh basil to the melted butter and garlic–delicious!

Spicy globe basil is a wonderfully aromatic basil that forms an exceptionally uniform eight to ten inch tall ball-shaped plant. The tiny leaves have an intense scent and a little goes a long way! A very decorative plant, excellent potted or for gardeners with limited space.

Cinnamon basil has a true cinnamon scent that makes it an excellent choice for herbal teas. The edible flowers are lavender with deep violet bracts and make a showy contrast in the garden.

Lettuce leaf basil is one of the oldest classic basils, this variety is aptly named for the voluminous size of its green leaves. Cut this mildly spicy sweet plant all summer by pruning back to a second set of leaves whenever you harvest.

Opal basil offers a fresh addition to salads and pastas. It makes an elegant, delicious opal-colored vinegar or jelly and its pink flowers and garnet-purple leaves are a pretty garnish for any cheese dip.

Basil is a member of the mint family and is often recommended for digestive complaints. Try an after dinner cup of basil tea.

SPINACH BASIL QUICHE

1 baked 9" pastry shell
1 12-ounce package frozen chopped spinach, thawed
1 tablespoon butter
1/3 cup chopped onion
3/4 cup half and half
2 large eggs
1/8 teaspoon ground black pepper
1 8-ounce container ricotta cheese
1 teaspoon fresh basil, chopped
nutmeg

Drain the thawed spinach, pressing out all the liquid. Melt the butter in a small skillet. Add the onion and cook for 3 minutes. Add the half and half and heat only until scalded. In a medium bowl, beat the eggs with the basil and pepper. Add the ricotta and beat until blended. Add the hot half and half and spinach and mix well. Pour into the baked shell. Sprinkle freshly grated nutmeg on top. Bake at 425 degrees for about 35 minutes. Cool to lukewarm before cutting.

TOMATO SCALLION SALAD

3 large ripe tomatoes
1/2 cup chopped scallions
1/4 cup chopped fresh basil
1/2 cup olive oil
3 tablespoons wine vinegar
freshly ground black pepper

Slice the tomatoes and arrange them on individual salad plates. Sprinkle with the scallions and the basil. Combine the oil and vinegar and shake well before pouring over the tomatoes. Sprinkle with the fresh pepper.

FRESH BASIL SALAD

bed of lettuce
tomato, cut in round slices
Swiss cheese, julienne strips
fresh basil leaves
2/3 cup olive oil
1/3 cup basil vinegar
1 tablespoon salad herbs
1 tablespoon lemon juice

Layer the tomato slices, Swiss cheese and basil leaves on the bed of lettuce. Combine the olive oil, vinegar, salad herbs, and lemon juice. Shake well. Garnish the salad with a fresh borage flower.

PISTOU (BASIL SOUP)

4 shallots, finely chopped
3 large garlic cloves, crushed
3 tablespoons vegetable oil
2 cans condensed tomato soup
2 cups water
2 teaspoons butter
2 tablespoons basil (dried)
1 1/2 cups cooked vermicelli
1/2 cup cheese croutons
fresh parsley for garnish
1 1/2 cups cooked green beans

Sauté shallots and garlic in the oil. Add soup and water. Sauté
the beans in the butter and basil. Add the beans and the cooked
noodles to the soup. Simmer for 5 minutes. Pour into hot
bowls. Sprinkle with croutons and fresh parsley. Serves 6.

PESTO

3/4 cup pine nuts or walnuts
2 cups packed fresh basil
1/8 teaspoon ground black pepper
1/2 cup grated parmesan cheese
1/2 cup grated romano cheese
2 large cloves garlic, peeled and quartered
1/2 cup olive oil

In a blender or food processor, combine the nuts, basil, pepper,
cheeses and garlic. Blend at high speed, just until smooth.
Gradually pour in the oil and continue to process until smooth.
Serve over pasta. This mixture can be frozen for up to five
months. To serve pesto as a dip, combine it with sour cream or
plain yogurt. Serve with assorted raw vegetables.

BASIL BEAN SOUP

1/2 pound dried white kidney beans
6 cups water
3 medium zucchini, diced
3 large potatoes, peeled and diced
6 medium carrots, peeled and thinly sliced
2 celery stalks, thinly sliced
2 onions, coarsely chopped
4 whole cloves
1 bay leaf
1 17-ounce can whole tomatoes, undrained
5 tablespoons fresh basil, snipped
4 drops Tabasco sauce

Soak the beans overnight in cold water to cover. Drain and
rinse in cold water. Place in a large pan and add the 6 cups of
water. Bring to a boil and add all the vegetables. Place the
cloves and bay leaf in a muslin bag and add to the pot. Add the
tomatoes, 3 tablespoons of the basil, and the Tabasco sauce.
Reduce heat and simmer until the beans are tender, about
2 1/2 hours. When serving, sprinkle with the remaining
2 tablespoons basil.

CREAMED MUSHROOMS AND SHRIMP

1 pound fresh mushrooms
1/4 cup butter
1/4 cup flour
2 cups milk
1/2 teaspoon herb salt
1 1/2 teaspoons dried basil
1/4 teaspoon pepper
1 cup shrimp
6 patty shells, precooked

Slice the mushrooms. Melt the butter in a skillet and cook the mushrooms just until tender. Sprinkle the flour on the mushrooms, mix well. Gradually add the milk, stirring constantly, until thickened. Add the herb salt, pepper, basil, and the shrimp and heat thoroughly. Serve hot in heated patty shells. Garnish with fresh slices of tomatoes and mushroom.

HAM ROLL-UPS WITH FRESH BASIL

8 ounces cream cheese, softened
3 tablespoons sweet red pepper relish
1/2 cup fresh basil, minced
ham slices

Combine the cream cheese, relish, and basil. Spread this mixture on ham slices, roll up jelly-roll style and cut into 1/2 inch pieces. Serve on toothpicks and garnish with fresh basil leaves and borage blossoms for a touch of color!

TOMATO SPREAD WITH HERBS

1 cup cottage cheese
2 tablespoons tomato paste
2 tablespoons milk
1 tablespoon salad oil
2 tablespoons chopped walnuts
2 teaspoons chopped shallots
2 teaspoons finely chopped fresh basil
2 teaspoons finely chopped fresh chives
2 teaspoons finely chopped fresh parsley
2 teaspoons lemon juice

Mix the tomato paste with the milk and add the oil gradually.
Add the cottage cheese and blend well. Add all the other ingredients and mix thoroughly. Serve with bread sticks for dipping.

PESTO SAUCE

2 tablespoons dried basil
1/3 cup ground walnuts
1/3 cups chopped fresh parsley
1 tablespoon minced shallots
2 garlic cloves
1 cup olive oil
1/3 cup grated parmesan

Combine all in a blender and mix until smooth.

A MENU FOR AUGUST

Sour Cream Herb Mix

Zucchini Soup

Banana Date Bread

Spanish Salad with Lemon Garlic Dressing

Shrimp Curry

Cardamon Bars

SOUR CREAM HERB MIX

1 cup sour cream
1 teaspoon, finely chopped, of each of the following herbs:
chives
thyme
dill
basil
rosemary
parsley
tarragon
lovage

Mix well and season with some freshly grated pepper. Serve with crackers, chips or pretzels.

ZUCCHINI SOUP

2 pounds zucchini, washed and thinly sliced
1/3 cup butter
1 medium onion, chopped
3 1/2 cups chicken broth
1/2 cup light cream
1/2 teaspoon nutmeg
pepper to taste

Sauté onion and zucchini in butter until limp. Add chicken broth, cover and simmer for 15 minutes. Put through blender to puree. Add cream, nutmeg and pepper. Serve hot or chill overnight.

BANANA DATE BREAD

3 1/2 cups flour
3 teaspoons baking powder
1 teaspoon salt
1 teaspoon baking soda
2 cups mashed, ripe bananas
1/2 cup chopped dates
2 tablespoons lemon juice
3/4 cup shortening
1 1/2 cups sugar
3 eggs
3/4 cup milk
1/2 cup chopped walnuts

Mix together the dry ingredients. Mash the bananas and add the lemon juice to them. Cream the shortening and sugar, add the eggs and beat thoroughly until very light and fluffy. Add the dry ingredients alternately with the milk. Fold in the bananas, dates and nuts. Pour into 2 greased loaf pans. Bake at 350 degrees for 1 hour, or until tests done. Cool in pans for 10 minutes, then remove and cool on wire racks.

SPANISH SALAD WITH LEMON-GARLIC DRESSING

Mixed salad greens, torn into bite-size pieces
1 large onion, thinly sliced and separated into rings
1 can mandarin orange slices

In a large salad bowl, toss the salad greens, onion and orange slices. Pour *Lemon-Garlic Dressing over the salad, toss again and serve immediately.

*Lemon-Garlic Dressing
1/2 cup olive oil
1/2 cup lemon juice
2 cloves garlic, crushed
freshly ground pepper

In a small bowl, combine the oil, lemon juice, garlic and pepper.

SHRIMP CURRY

2 tablespoons butter
1 1/2 cups finely chopped, peeled tart apples
2 tablespoons flour
2 teaspoons curry powder
2 cups milk
2 cups cleaned, cooked shrimp
hot, cooked rice

Melt butter, add the apples and cook for 5 minutes. Combine the flour, and curry powder. Stir into the apples. Add milk slowly. Cook and stir until thick. Add the shrimp and heat gently. Serve over rice and garnish with paprika.

CARDAMON BARS

1/2 cup butter
1/2 cup brown sugar
1 teaspoon salt
1 cup flour
2 teaspoons ground cardamon seed
2 eggs, well beaten
1 cup brown sugar
1 teaspoon vanilla
2 tablespoons flour
1/2 teaspoon baking powder
1 1/2 cups shredded coconut
1 cup chopped walnuts

Mix together the butter, 1/2 cup brown sugar and salt. Blend in 1 cup flour and the cardamon. Spread mixture in an 8" x 12" pan. Bake at 325 degrees for 15 minutes. Add 1 cup brown sugar and vanilla to the eggs and beat until thick and foamy. Add the 2 tablespoons flour, baking powder, coconut, and walnuts. Mix well and spread over the baked mixture. Return to oven and bake at 325 degrees for 25 minutes. Cool and cut into bars.

SEPTEMBER

The morns are meeker than they were,
The nuts are getting brown,
The berries cheek is plumper,
The rose is out of town.
The maple wears a gayer scarf,
The field a scarlet gown,
Lest I should be old-fashioned
I'll put a trinket on.

Autumn
Emily Dickinson

Traditionally, Michaelmas Day was celebrated on September 29th and honored the archangel St. Michael. The festival signified the end of the harvest time in Medieval Europe. It is one of the four quarters of the year when rents and bills came due, and often a goose was included in the payment of rent to the landlord!

In England, a large glove was suspended from a pole on the town hall to signal that the Michaelmas Fair was to begin. Merchants and craftsmen came from miles around to sell their wares.

A Michaelmas feast must include a roasted goose, for it was believed that "if you eat goose on St. Michaelmas Day you will never want money all the year round!"

Ginger was traditionally served in at least one of the feast dishes. St. Michael was believed to be a healer and guardian, and medieval physicians considered ginger to be a healing herb and important for protection against infection.

The New England Aster blooms at the time of the Michaelmas Feast and is known as the Michaelmas Daisy.

September, and the scent of ripening grapes is in the air. The first tart apples are ready and we bring a bushel into the shop for customers to munch on as they browse.

Back into the greenhouse come the tender herbs and scented geraniums, overflowing their pots with their summer growth, and ready to give us winter cuttings. The greenhouse is restocked with plants for winter windowsills – chives, rosemary, tarragon, thyme, scented geraniums and sweet bay.

The silver king artemisia is ripe for picking now that the tiny seed heads have formed, and large bunches hang from the rafters. The top of the barn is filled with summer's bounty, and the colors of the drying flowers and herbs is glorious – deep purple and yellow statice, white everlasting and yarrow, magenta oregano blossoms, pink chives, and orange-yellow goldenrod.

Teasel stands in tall baskets with dock and other brown grasses from the fields, and smaller baskets hold rosehips and seedpods.

It is now that we begin making our herbal wreaths, stuffing the wreath wires with silver king and mugwort, then decorating them with colorful dried flowers, seedpods and spices – cinnamon sticks, whole nutmeg and ginger root.

Tiny bird nests are filled with dried bouquets, and our imaginations run wild with this new bounty of materials to work with!

Already we are thinking ahead and planning for the holidays soon to come.

DILL
Annual
anethum graveolens

Dill is a tall, graceful plant growing up to three feet on a single stalk with feathery branches, called "dill weed." Pale yellow flowerheads appear which form flat seed heads. Dill is a native of Europe and belongs to the parsley family.

Dill should be sown outside where it is to remain. Dill prefers full sun and rich soil. Several sowings can be made during the summer for a continuous supply of dill weed. The plant often self-sows.

Dill weed can be harvested early in the summer and dried in a basket or on a very fine screen. The oven may be used for quick drying in humid weather.

In the Middle Ages, dill was thought to be abhorred by witches and was used against them in witchcraft. Hang a sprig of dill in your doorway to discourage any witches lurking about!

The name dill comes from the Norse word "Dilla" which means "to lull." At Pickity Place we fill a small pillow with dill seeds to help lull baby to sleep.

Dill and fennel seeds were known as "go-to-meeting seeds," and were given to children to chew during long church services to keep them quiet. Carrying a bag of dried dill over the heart was thought to combat the spell of the "evil eye."

Dill is loved by honeybees. It is used as a base for pickles and makes a flavorful vinegar. The leaves make a handsome garnish. Dill leaves go well with sour cream or cottage cheese, as a flavoring for fish, or with egg dishes and salads. Use dill seed to flavor cabbage, onions, pastries, breads and sauces.

Dill is said to be stimulating to the appetite and settling to the stomach. To prepare an infusion, steep 2 teaspoons of seeds in 1 cup of water for 10-15 minutes. Take one half cup at a time, 1 or 2 cups per day.

Plant dill along the garden perimeter to attract bees or use

---

it as a backdrop for shorter plants. You may want to tie plants to a stake to keep them upright, since wind can destroy the tall stalks.

The freshly picked leaves can also be frozen. Simply snip off what is needed and return the rest to the freezer. Harvest the seeds when the flower matures, between two to three weeks after blossoming. An easy way is to cut the whole plant and place it seed head down in a paper bag to catch all the seeds. Hang in a dry area and the seeds will readily drop out.

For companion planting, dill is supposed to enhance the growth of cabbage, onions and lettuce. Dill appreciates a side dressing of dried cow manure or good compost when the plants are 4-6" tall.

ZUCCHINI WITH DILL

2 pounds zucchini
4 tablespoons butter
black pepper
2 tablespoons chopped fresh dill

Wash and slice the zucchini. Melt the butter and add the zucchini. Cook gently, covered, for 10 minutes or until tender. Add the dill and season with freshly ground black pepper.

DILL MAYONNAISE

1 cup sour cream
1/2 cup mayonnaise
1 tablespoon lemon juice
1/2 teaspoon celery seed
2 teaspoon dill weed

Mix all together well and chill. Very good as a dip for shrimp.

DILL BREAD

1 package dry yeast
1/4 cup warm water
1 tablespoon honey
1 tablespoon vegetable oil
1 teaspoon salt
1 egg, beaten
1/2 cup cottage cheese
1/2 cup yogurt
1 tablespoon onion, minced
1/4 teaspoon baking soda
2 tablespoons dill seeds
1 cup whole wheat flour
1 cup white flour

Sprinkle yeast over the warm water. Let stand for 10 minutes.
Add the remaining ingredients except the flours. Mix well. Add
the wheat flour and stir. Add the white flour. Beat 2 minutes.
Cover and let rise until doubled, about 2 hours. Punch down
and place in a buttered 2 quart round casserole. Bake at 350
degrees for 30 minutes. Cool on a wire rack.

CABBAGE AND DILL SALAD

1/2 head Chinese cabbage
1 cucumber
4 scallions, sliced
3 tablespoons olive oil
1 tablespoon dill vinegar
4 hard-boiled eggs
2 tablespoons chopped fresh dill

Cut the cabbage in thin strips and put in a large salad bowl.
Peel and slice the cucumber and add with the scallions to the
salad. Stir in the oil and vinegar and mix thoroughly. Shell the
eggs and slice them into rounds. Gently stir in the eggs and
the fresh dill.

SOUR CREAM CORN BREAD WITH DILL

2 cups cornmeal
2 tablespoons sugar
1 teaspoon salt
1 teaspoon baking soda
2 teaspoons baking powder
2 eggs
2 cups sour cream
1 tablespoon dill weed

Sift the dry ingredients together. Beat the eggs until frothy.
Add the sour cream to the eggs. Add to the dry ingredients and
mix well. Stir in the dill weed. Pour into greased 9" square pan
and bake at 400 degrees about 30 minutes. Serves 6-8.

DILL OATMEAL BREAD

1 package dry yeast
1/4 cup lukewarm water
4 cups boiling skim milk
2 cups oatmeal
1/4 cup butter
1/2 cup molasses
1 tablespoon salt
2 tablespoons dill seed
3/4 cup finely chopped onion
10-11 cups flour

Dissolve the yeast in the warm water. Add the hot skim milk to the oatmeal and butter and let stand 30 minutes. Add the molasses, salt, and dissolved yeast. Stir in the dill seed and onions. Add enough of the flour to make a soft dough. Place in a buttered bowl, cover and let rise until doubled. Turn out and knead on a floured board, about 10 minutes. Divide into 3 loaves and place in buttered loaf pans. Let rise again. Brush tops with melted butter. Bake at 400 degrees for 40-50 minutes.

DILL CHIVE BREAD

2 1/2 cups flour
1 package yeast
1/4 cup warm water
2 tablespoons sugar
1 tablespoon chopped fresh chives
2 tablespoons chopped fresh dill
1 teaspoon salt
1/4 teaspoon baking soda
1 cup cottage cheese
1 egg, lightly beaten
1 tablespoon butter

Dissolve the yeast in the warm water. Combine the yeast, sugar, herbs, salt and baking soda with 1 cup of the flour. Heat the cottage cheese with the butter until it is lukewarm. Add it to the yeast mixture. Add the beaten egg and stir well. Beat in the remaining flour to make a stiff dough. Cover and let stand in a warm place until doubled in bulk. Stir down and place in a buttered loaf pan. Let rise again. Bake at 350 degrees for 45 minutes. While still hot, brush with melted butter and sprinkle with dill seeds. Cool in pan for 15 minutes.

SOUR CREAM HERB BREAD

3 1/4 cups flour
1/4 cup sugar
1 teaspoon salt
1/2 teaspoon celery seed
1/2 teaspoon dill seed
1/2 teaspoon minced onion
2 packages dry yeast
1 cup sour cream
1/2 cup water
3 tablespoons butter
1 egg

Combine 2 cups flour, salt, sugar, seeds, onion and yeast. In saucepan heat sour cream, water and 3 tablespoons butter until very warm. Add warm liquid and egg to flour mixture. Blend at low speed until moistened; beat for 3 minutes at medium speed. By hand, stir in remaining 1 1/4 cups flour. Cover and let rise until doubled. Stir down dough. Turn into greased loaf pan. Cover and let rise for 30-45 minutes. Bake at 350 degrees for 35-40 minutes until golden brown. Brush warm loaf with butter and sprinkle with toasted sesame seed.

CREAMY DILL DIP

1 cup sour cream
1/4 cup mayonnaise
1 1/4 teaspoon celery salt
1 tablespoon dill weed
1 1/2 teaspoon parsley flakes
1/4 teaspoon onion powder
1 clove garlic, minced
1/2 teaspoon prepared horseradish

Combine all and chill at least 2 hours. Serve with fresh vegetables for dipping.

CUCUMBERS IN SOUR CREAM

2 medium cucumbers
1 cup sour cream
2 tablespoons lemon juice
1/8 cup fresh dill leaves
lettuce

Slice the cucumbers very thin and toss with the other ingredients. Refrigerate at least 1 hour. Serve on a bed of lettuce and sprinkle with paprika.

DEVILED EGG SALAD

6 eggs, hard boiled
1/4 teaspoon dill weed
1/4 teaspoon celery seed
1 shallot, finely chopped
freshly grated ginger root
freshly ground pepper
pimento

Carefully peel the eggs, split in half lengthwise and remove
yolks. Mash the yolks and add the remaining ingredients except
the pimento. Stuff the egg halves and top with the bit of pimento. Sprinkle with a bit of paprika. Serve on a bed of lettuce
with a tomato round.

DILL CHERVIL DRESSING

1 cup sour cream
1 teaspoon vegetable oil
1 teaspoon dried chervil
1 teaspoon dried dill weed

Blend together thoroughly.

LAMB CASSEROLE

2 pounds lamb shoulder, cut for stew
1/2 stick butter
1 pound green beans, cut in 1" pieces
2 large onions, sliced
1 cup chicken stock
2 tablespoons fresh dill, chopped
2 teaspoons paprika
pepper to taste

Brown meat in butter in casserole. Add remaining ingredients and season with the pepper. Cover and bake at 350 degrees until meat is tender, about 1 1/2 hours. Garnish with chopped mint.

SPINACH PIE WITH DILL

2 pounds spinach leaves, washed and torn
2 8-ounce cans refrigerated crescent dinner rolls
1/2 cup finely chopped onion
3 teaspoons dill weed
2 cups feta cheese, crumbled
1 cup creamed cottage cheese
2 eggs, slightly beaten

Cover spinach with boiling water and let stand 5 minutes stirring once. Drain well. Unroll one can of dough into 2 long rectangles. Place in ungreased 13" x 9" baking pan. Press over bottom and 1/2" up sides to form crust. Bake at 400 degrees for 5 minutes. Combine drained spinach, onion, dill weed, feta cheese, cottage cheese and eggs. Mix well and spread over partially baked crust. Unroll second can of dough into 2 long rectangles, 13" x 5". Place over spinach mixture. Bake for 20-30 minutes.

BAKED MATZOH, CHICKEN AND DILL CASSEROLE

6 eggs
2 tablespoons dried dill
1/4 cup finely chopped fresh parsley
3 cups cooked chicken, cut into strips 1/4" x 1 1/2" long
fresh ground black pepper
1/2 cup vegetable oil
3 plain squares matzoh
2 cups chicken stock, fat skimmed off
1/2 cup finely chopped onions

Beat the eggs until frothy, add the onions, dill, parsley and the pepper. Add the chicken. Mix well together until the chicken is coated. Heat 1 teaspoon oil in an 8" square shallow baking dish, tilting to spread it evenly. Dip a matzoh into the chicken stock until well moistened. Lay it in the baking dish, spread half the chicken and egg mixture evenly over it, moisten a second matzoh in the chicken stock and place it over the chicken. Repeat with the remaining chicken and matzoh. Pour 1/4 cup oil evenly over the top matzoh and bake for 25 minutes longer. Serve at once.

LEMON OLIVE MEATBALLS

1 pound ground beef
3 tablespoons lemon juice
1 tablespoon herb salt
4 ounces sharp cheddar, grated
12 small green olives, finely chopped
1/4 green pepper, finely chopped
1 cup herb seasoned bread crumbs
1 egg
1/4 cup milk
12-15 slices bacon, partially cooked

Mix together the beef, lemon juice and herb salt. Add the grated cheese, olives, pepper, bread crumbs, milk and egg. Shape into small balls and wrap each with 1/3 slice of the partially cooked bacon and secure with a toothpick. Bake at 375 degrees for 20-25 minutes. Serve hot.

STUFFED MUSHROOM CAPS

1 pounds large fresh mushrooms
1/2 cup butter, melted
1/4 cup finely chopped Egyptian onion stalks
1/4 cup semi-sweet white wine
1 cup herb bread crumbs, crushed

Brush the mushrooms. Remove the stems and finely shop them.
Melt the butter in a skillet. Dip the caps in the butter and place
crown side down in a shallow pan. Saute the chopped mushrooms and onions in the remaining butter. Remove from heat
and add the wine and bread crumbs. Mix lightly and spoon
onto the mushroom caps. Bake at 350 degrees for 10-15
minutes.

A MENU FOR SEPTEMBER

Roquefort Cognac Dip

Tomato Leek Soup

Pumpkin Seed Muffins

September Salad

Cabbage Rolls

Gingered Corn

Spiced Apple Cakes

ROQUEFORT COGNAC DIP

3 ounces Roquefort cheese
2 tablespoons butter, softened
2 tablespoons brandy
3 red apples; we like Delicious
lemon juice

Mix together the cheese, softened butter and brandy. Refrigerate overnight for the flavors to blend. Core the apples but leave them unpeeled. Dip 1/2" slices of the apples in lemon juice and arrange on a platter around the bowl for dipping.

TOMATO LEEK SOUP

2 onions, diced
2 leeks, sliced thin
1 clove garlic, minced
1/4 cup olive oil
2 tablespoons parsley, chopped
1 teaspoon thyme, crushed
1 bay leaf
2 cups tomatoes, fresh or canned
3 cups chicken or beef stock
soy sauce

Sauté onions, leeks and garlic in olive oil until transparent. Add the herbs, tomatoes and stock and simmer over medium heat until flavors are combined. Remove bay leaf. Season with soy sauce and garnish with green onion tops.

PUMPKIN SEED MUFFINS

1 3/4 cups flour
1/2 cup sugar
1/4 cup toasted, shelled pumpkin seeds, chopped
3 teaspoons baking powder
1 1/2 teaspoons cinnamon
1/2 teaspoon salt
3/4 cup milk
1/2 cup canned or cooked pumpkin
1/3 cup oil
1 egg, beaten

Combine flour, sugar, pumpkin seeds, baking powder, cinnamon and salt. In small bowl, combine remaining ingredients. Stir into dry ingredients just until moistened. (Batter will be lumpy.) Spoon batter evenly into 12 greased muffin cups. Bake at 400 degrees for 20-25 minutes. Serve warm.

SEPTEMBER SALAD

Arrange sliced cucumbers and tomatoes on a bed of Boston lettuce. Mince together 1 tablespoon each of the following fresh herbs and add: lovage, tarragon, parsley, and calendula petals. Sprinkle with mozzarella cheese. Serve with Herb Cheese Dressing (see index).

CABBAGE ROLLS

12 large cabbage leaves
1 1/2 pounds ground beef
1 grated carrot
1 cup finely minced cabbage
1/4 cup grated onion
1/4 teaspoon pepper
2 teaspoons sweet marjoram, dried
1/2 cup soft bread crumbs
1/4 cup water
2 eggs, beaten
1/3 cup butter
1/4 cup honey
1/4 cup molasses
3 tablespoons water

Steam the cabbage leaves to soften them. Combine beef, carrot, minced cabbage, onion, pepper, sweet marjoram, bread crumbs, 1/4 cup water and eggs. Mix well. Use to fill the cabbage leaves, rolling into cylinders. Place rolls, seam side down in baking dish. Blend together butter, honey, molasses and water. Pour over the rolls and bake at 350 degrees about 45 minutes.

GINGERED CORN

4 cups cooked corn, drained
2 tablespoons butter
1 teaspoon olive oil
1 onion, minced
1 teaspoon finely chopped garlic
2 tablespoons fresh ginger root, peeled and finely chopped
1/2 teaspoon ground hot red pepper
1/4 teaspoon ground black pepper

Combine the butter and olive oil. Add the onion and sauté it until it wilts. Add the ginger root and garlic and sauté for 1 minute. Add the corn and sprinkle on the peppers. Stir to mix. Heat gently to flavor the corn.

SPICED APPLE CAKES

3 cups chopped apples
2 cups sugar
2 tablespoons cinnamon
1 teaspoon nutmeg
3 cups flour
1 teaspoon baking soda
3 eggs, beaten
1 cup vegetable oil
2 teaspoons vanilla
1 cup chopped walnuts

Toss the apples with the spices. Add the flour and soda. In a small bowl, combine the eggs, oil and vanilla. Add to the first mixture. Fold in the walnuts. Batter will be quite stiff. Pour into a 13" x 14" greased pan. Bake at 350 degrees for 30-40 minutes. Cut into squares and top with real whipped cream and a sprig of lemon balm.

OCTOBER

I keep a goat to see him prance
I carry a staff, I talk to my plants
I stare in the fire and crook my thumb
and whatever I see in the flames, I become.

Halloween is the end of the year in the ancient Pagan Celtic calendar, and was called Summer's End or "Samhain."

October brings to mind piles of glowing pumpkins, baskets overflowing with nuts and fruits, and a warming cup of hot mulled cider.

Halloween is the holiday signaling the entrance into winter, and October is the time when ghosts, spirits, and witches were thought to be most powerful and most lonely. Early witches wore capes of purple to suggest the darkness, which they loved, or dark blue to represent the night in which they worked their spells.

A witch's broom was always made of ash and bound with willow twigs. In ancient Greece, celery seeds were thought to keep witches from falling off their brooms!

The first frost has come, and each night we must cover the orange mound of pumpkins piled in the old wagon. On sunny days, the hillsides are ablaze in their autumn finery, and a brisk walk along the path in the woods is exhilarating!

The old wood-burning cookstove is keeping us warm and cozy in the shop, and a pot of hot mulled cider bubbling on top greets guests coming in from the cold. Old friends are coming by for their stock of winter herbs and spices and perhaps a dried bouquet to liven up the winter months ahead.

Out come the brown checked tablecloths in the dining room, and the mantle is decorated with bittersweet, apples, nuts, pumpkins and gourds. Braided Indian Corn decorates one wall and an herbal wreath in brown and gold tones another.

Halloween is one of our favorite holidays, and crossed sticks in the form of "witches crofts" are hung in the windows. Corn husks, dried and then dyed black, are crafted into witches, with cornsilk for hair. The old black velvet cape hangs on a peg by the door, beside the broom with the twisted handle.

The Witch's Garden has been trimmed back, and the ancient cauldron hangs from its tripod against the stone wall.

We have started making pomander balls, filling apples and oranges with whole cloves. These are rolled in a spicy mixture and put by the woodstove to dry. A cricket has come in from the cold, and we let him stay for good luck!

The gardens are looking stark now, but we still enjoy the texture of the grey santolina and the southernwood as it waves gracefully. It is time to think about mulching the lavenders and putting them to bed for the winter.

SUMMER SAVORY

Annual

satureia hortensis

Summer savory is a fast-growing herb, growing to about one foot in height. The green leaves are narrow and needle-shaped. The flowers, which appear in July, are light pink to lavender.

Savory prefers light, well-drained soil and full sun. Keep the plant moist during dry weather. Summer savory is a slow starter, but can be grown from seed. A bit of mulch placed under the plant will keep the leaves clean for harvesting.

Summer savory may be harvested two or three times during the summer. Its flavor is best before the flowers form. It may be dried on screens or hung in bunches. When the herb is crisp dry, remove the leaves from the stem and store in tight containers.

Honey bees are attracted to summer savory when it is in blossom. An old remedy for a bee sting suggests rubbing the spot with fresh savory leaves after removing the stinger.

Vinegar made from summer savory is delicious or try making savory butter for a tasty spread.

Savory is known as the "bean herb" because of its affinity for all kinds of cooked beans. It is excellent for flavoring seafood sauces and bean soups. Add it to salad dressings, or brew it for a tasty tea.

Summer savory tastes like a spicy thyme and blends well with most flavors, acting as a catalyst to bring them together.

WINTER SAVORY

Hardy Perennial
saturcia montana

Winter Savory is a compact bush, with narrow dark green leaves. Its height is usually no more than twelve inches. Winter savory makes an ideal hedge to surround the herb garden. It was a favored plant for this purpose during the Tudor days in England.

The plant prefers sunny, well-drained soil. Propagation is by seed or by tip cutting of new growth in late spring.

Dry the winter savory by hanging it in bunches and then stripping off the leaves. When dried, the flavor is not as pungent and good as the annual variety, summer savory.

The savories are native to the Mediterranean area, and their history goes back to ancient times. Virgil wrote that it was among the most fragrant of herbs, and suggested that it be planted around beehives.

Use winter savory interchangeably with summer savory in recipes. Try winter savory whenever you want a slightly peppery taste.

Winter savory can be grown in a container, bringing it inside in winter. Scant watering is necessary as too much moisture in the soil can cause winterkill. Winter savory is a short-lived plant and will need to be replaced with new plants every 2 or 3 years.

BEAN AND BACON SALAD

2 pounds green beans
4 bacon slices, cooked and crumbled
1 tablespoon scallions, chopped
1/4 cup sweet red pepper, chopped
1/2 cup olive oil
1 tablespoon savory vinegar
1 tablespoon lemon juice
1 tablespoon fresh parsley, minced
2 tablespoons fresh summer savory, minced
1 teaspoon sugar
pepper to taste

Cook the green beans in 1" of boiling water for 15 minutes or
until crisp tender. Drain. Sauté the scallions and red pepper in
2 tablespoons of the bacon fat. Add to the beans. In a small pan,
heat the oil, vinegar, lemon juice, herbs and sugar to boiling.
Pour this over the beans and toss to coat evenly. Pour into a
serving dish and sprinkle with the crumbled bacon.

SAVORY BROWN RICE

3 cups water
1/2 teaspoon salt
1 cup brown rice, rinsed
1 cup onion, finely chopped
1 tablespoon olive oil
1 tablespoon fresh parsley, chopped
1 teaspoon fresh summer savory, chopped

Bring the water to a boil, add the salt and rice. Return to boil,
cover pan, then simmer for 35 to 45 minutes until the rice has
absorbed the water. Sauté the onion in the oil until golden. Add
the herbs and combine with the rice. Keep warm until serving.

GREEN BEANS WITH SAVORY

1 pound green beans
2 teaspoons fresh savory, chopped
4 tablespoons sour cream
2 teaspoons Egyptian onion stalk, chopped

Cook the beans until tender. Drain. Add the savory, onion and sour cream. Cover and heat gently. Serve hot.

HOT POTATO SALAD

1 1/2 pounds new potatoes
2 tablespoons finely chopped scallions
3 tablespoons olive oil
1 tablespoon savory vinegar
1 tablespoon fresh summer savory, minced
2 tablespoons chopped chives
black pepper

Wash the potatoes and cook them in their skins. Peel as soon as they are cool enough to handle. Cut into quarters and stir in the chopped scallions. Pour over the oil and vinegar and mix gently. Stir in the summer savory and freshly ground pepper. Scatter the chives over the top of the salad.

GREEN BEAN BUNDLES

1 pound cooked French cut green beans
pimento
1 tablespoon lemon juice
1/4 teaspoon salt
pepper
3 tablespoons olive oil
2 teaspoons dried summer savory

Arrange the beans in individual servings in bundles; drape a piece of pimento across the bundle. Combine the remaining ingredients and pour over the beans.

HERB FRENCH DRESSING

1 teaspoon dried summer savory
1 teaspoon dried crushed rosemary
1 teaspoon dried basil
1 cup olive oil
1/2 cup basil vinegar
2 teaspoons dry mustard
1/4 cup water

Crush the herbs in a mortar with a pestle, then shake all ingredients together. Serve with a salad of lettuce, fresh mushrooms and alfalfa sprouts.

SAVORY GREEN BEANS

1 1/2 pounds green beans, rinsed and broken in half
2-3 sprigs savory, rinsed and patted dry
1 tablespoon chopped fresh thyme leaves
1 tablespoon chopped fresh rosemary
1/2 cup grated parmesan cheese
4 tablespoons butter or margarine

In a saucepan, cover the beans with water, add the savory and bring to a boil. Cover and simmer for 20 minutes. Place the beans in a warm serving bowl, sprinkle with the thyme and rosemary and toss well. Sprinkle on the Parmesan cheese and toss again. In a small skillet, melt the butter and heat until it browns a little. Pour over the beans and serve.

A MENU FOR OCTOBER

Apple Walnut Soup

Bannock Cakes

Orange-Beet Salad

Broccoli Strudel

Pumpkin Nut Roll

Mulled Cider

APPLE WALNUT SOUP

3 green or tart apples, unpeeled, cored and diced
1 small white turnip, trimmed but unpeeled
2 ounces sweet cider mixed with 2 ounces applejack
2 cups water
1 cup apple juice
pinch each of cinnamon and cloves
1/4 teaspoon pepper
1/2 teaspoon sugar
juice of 1/2 lemon
2 slices bacon, diced
4 tablespoons walnuts, finely ground

Combine all ingredients but the walnuts, and simmer uncovered for 30 minutes. Puree in the blender until smooth. Strain into a saucepan, add 1/2 the walnuts and bring to a boil. Allow to cool and then chill thoroughly. Serve chilled, with the remaining walnuts as a garnish.

BANNOCK CAKES

1 cup cornmeal
1 cup oatmeal
1 cup buttermilk
grated rind of 1 lemon
2 tablespoons melted butter
2 tablespoons honey
1/2 teaspoon ginger, ground
1 teaspoon baking soda

Mix all ingredients in the order given. Heat 1 tablespoon oil in an iron skillet. Pour in the batter and cook for 10 minutes, then transfer to a 375 degree oven for 20 minutes. Cut in wedges and serve hot.

ORANGE-BEET SALAD

1 11-ounce can mandarin orange slices, chilled and drained
1 cup julienne beets, chilled and drained
1 apple, cored and sliced
1/4 cup salad oil
2 tablespoons frozen orange juice concentrate, thawed
1 tablespoon lemon juice
1/2 teaspoon dry mustard
Boston lettuce

In a screwtop jar combine oil, juice concentrate, lemon juice, dry mustard; cover, shake well and chill. At serving time, layer the lettuce with the oranges, beets and apple slices. Drizzle the dressing over all.

BROCCOLI STRUDEL

8 cups chopped broccoli
1 cup onion, chopped
1/2 cup chopped walnuts
1 cup grated Swiss cheese
1 egg
1 1/2 cups bread crumbs
1 teaspoon Fines Herbes
5 sheets phyllo
butter, melted

Sauté the broccoli and the onions in a bit of butter. Mix well with the herbs, walnuts, bread crumbs, cheese and egg. Butter the sheets of phyllo and stack them. Spread the filling on top of the phyllo, fold in the ends and roll up jellyroll fashion. Bake at 375 degrees until browned. Serve with *Wine Sauce.

*Wine Sauce
1/4 cup butter
4 tablespoons flour
3/4 cup white wine
1 1/2 cups light cream
salt and white pepper to taste

Melt the butter but do not brown it. Remove from heat and add
the flour. Stir with a whisk until smooth, adding the wine.
Return to heat and stir until it begins to thicken. Quickly add
1/2 cup cream. Lower the heat and continue stirring. As the
sauce begins to thicken, add the remaining cream. If necessary,
add up to 1/2 cup more cream to achieve desired thickness.
Season with the salt and pepper.

PUMPKIN NUT ROLL

3 eggs
1 cup sugar
2/3 cup pumpkin
1 teaspoon lemon juice
3/4 cup flour
1/2 teaspoon ginger
1 teaspoon baking powder
2 teaspoon cinnamon
1/2 teaspoon nutmeg
1 cup chopped nuts

Beat the eggs 5 minutes at high speed. Gradually beat in the
sugar. Stir in the pumpkin and lemon juice. Stir together the
dry ingredients and fold them into the pumpkin mixture. Line
a jellyroll pan with waxed paper and spread the mixture. Top
with the walnuts. Bake at 375 degrees for 15 minutes. Turn the
cake out onto a linen towel, dusted with confectioners sugar.
Start at narrow end and roll towel and cake together. Cool

thoroughly. Unroll, spread with *Filling, roll up and chill.

*Filling:
1 cup powdered sugar
8 ounces cream cheese
4 tablespoons butter
1/2 teaspoon vanilla
1 cup Cool Whip

Beat all together until smooth.

MULLED CIDER

1/2 cup sugar
1 1/2 cups water
3 strips lemon peel
3-inch cinnamon stick
10 whole cloves

Boil all ingredients together for 10 minutes. Strain, and add 3 pints of cider. Heat but do not boil. Serve hot with a bit of grated nutmeg.

NOVEMBER

In the other gardens
And all up the vale
From the autumn bonfires
See the smoke trail!
Pleasant summer over
And all the summer flowers,
The red fire blazes,
The grey smoke towers.
Sing a song of seasons!
Something bright in all!
Flowers in the summer,
Fires in the fall!

Autumn Fires
Robert Lewis Stevenson

Martinmas, traditionally celebrated on November 11th, is a feast day of St. Martin, a patron saint of the French. Martinmas falls at the end of the harvest season and is celebrated with feasts and new wine. In ancient Europe, the children received apples and nuts. Harvesters paraded through the streets carrying lanterns and singing.

St. Catherine's Day is also celebrated in November. The wheel is the symbol of her death in the 14th century. Flaming wheels of fire were whirled by a juggler. These were called "Catherine Wheels." Above the feast table was hung a chandelier, over a frothy pot of hot mulled cider and apples. This was the "Cathern" bowl.

As you prepare for the holidays, put some mugwort in your shoes to keep your feet rested. It is known as the "herb for the weary traveler!"

Leaves rustle under the eaves, the days are short, and the first damp smell of snow is in the air. Helpers come in with loads of wood and their noses are red!

We are busy, busy, busy making herbal "goodies" for the holidays. The shop is filling up with gifts – mortors filled with herbs and tied with a calico bow; mugwort pillows for dreaming on; bags of woodstove incense and herbal soaps in baskets tied up with pretty ribbons. Hand-dipped candles scented with bayberry or cranberry hang from an old wagon wheel. We are aging 25 pounds of Christmas Pine Potpourri for holiday shoppers, and the larger rosemary plants have been trimmed to sell as miniature Christmas Trees.

Our shelves are stocked with spices and herbs for holiday baking: cardamon for sweet breads, anise for Springerle cookies, and vanilla beans for making your own Kahlua. We bring out the candied angelica and real licorice sticks.

Now that the winter winds are whistling in the chimney, we take pleasure in seeing the wood, all split and stacked in the barn.

This is the time of year when we are most busy with our mail order catalog, and stacks of boxes are lined up by the kitchen door, waiting for their journey to eager recipients. We must take time out from this rush and be thankful that we are busy!

SAGE

Hardy Perennial
salvia officinalis

Sage grows to a foot or more in height, has a rather square stem and oblong, hairy leaves. The flowers are purplish blue. The leaves turn grey as they mature. Sage plants need to be replaced every three or four years, as the stems become woody and tough.

Sage requires a sunny spot with poor, well-drained soil. Plants may be started easily from seed. Plant the seeds a foot apart to allow ample room for growth.

Harvest sage in late summer, clipping only stems that are high up on the plant. Do not cut into the woody sections of the plant. Store the whole leaves and crumble them as needed.

Sage comes from the Latin word meaning "to heal" or "to be well." It was long thought to prolong life and made one sage and wise. It has a reputation for restoring bad memory! Sage thrives in New England, and of course the Vermonters use it when making their sage cheese. Sage is one of the most popular herbs today – we all know it as an indispensable seasoning for Thanksgiving dinner.

Sage is considered a powerful bactericide and can be sewn into sachets and placed in closets to repel insects. It was used by the American Indians as a mouth cleanser. Sage is said to aid in the digestibility of heavy, greasy meats.

The Chinese were so enamoured with sage that they were willing to trade tea for sage in a ratio of 4 to 1! Try brewing sage tea for a spring tonic, and sweeten it with a bit of maple syrup.

To counteract richness, use sage when cooking goose, duck, pork or oily fish. It goes well with onions, cheese or egg dishes, stuffing, or rich cream sauces.

Purple sage, *s. officinalis 'purpurea'*, has deep purple foliage and is a pleasing contrast in the garden. Use it in stuffings, sausage, omelets and soups.

Dwarf sage, *s. officinalis 'dwarf'*, is a more compact grower with a smaller leaf. It makes a good rock garden or container plant.

Clary sage, *s. sclarea*, is an unusual and showy biennial sage with huge grey leaves and beautiful lilac and pink flowers. The scent is balsam-like. The fresh or dried leaves can be used in the same ways as garden sage. The flowers make a lovely garnish. Clary does best in a poor, dry soil. The plants will flower in their second year and will readily selfsow.

Pineapple sage, *s. elegans*, is not hardy in New England, but makes a wonderful container-grown plant which can come in during winter months. The leaves give off a strong pineapple scent and flavor and make a heady tea. Scarlet flowers appear in late summer.

Sage is a beautiful and aromatic shrub, popular with bees and valuable as a flowering garden plant.

Plant sage with cabbages, carrots and tomatoes, but not near onions.

MICHAELMAS CHICKEN

1 8-ounce package herb-seasoned stuffing mix
3 cups cooked chicken, sliced
1/2 cup butter
1/2 cup flour
dash pepper
2 tablespoons herbs for chicken and fish
4 cups chicken broth
6 slightly beaten eggs
1 can evaporated milk
1/4 cup milk
1 cup sour cream
1/4 cup chopped pimento

Prepare stuffing mix according to package directions in a
3 quart casserole. Arrange chicken slices over top. Melt butter
in a skillet. Add flour, pepper and broth stirring constantly. Add
the eggs and mix well. Pour over the chicken mixture. Bake at
325 degrees for 45 minutes to 1 hour. Combine remaining
ingredients and heat until smooth. Serve over the casserole.

SAGE BREAD

1 package dry yeast
1/4 cup warm water
2 tablespoons shortening
2 tablespoons sugar
2 teaspoons caraway seeds
1 tablespoon fresh sage, finely chopped
2 1/3 cups flour

In a large bowl dissolve the yeast in warm water. Add the shortening, sugar, caraway and sage and mix well. Add the flour and
stir until smooth. Cover and let rise until double. Stir down and
pour into a buttered loaf pan. Bake at 375 degrees for 45-50
minutes. Cover with foil if top browns too quickly.

APPLE SAGE JELLY

3 cups apple juice
1/2 cup fresh sage, chopped
2 tablespoons cider vinegar
3 cups sugar
1/2 cup liquid pectin
sprigs of fresh sage

Bring 1 cup of apple juice to a rolling boil, pour it over the sage
and allow to seep for 20 minutes. Strain into a large saucepan.
Add the vinegar and the remaining 2 cups of apple juice. Mix in
the sugar and bring to a boil. Stir in the pectin and boil hard for
1 minute. Remove from heat and skim off foam with metal
spoon. Pour into hot, sterilized jars. Immerse a sprig of sage in
the jelly. Seal with paraffin.

SAGE STUFFING FOR POULTRY

3/4 cup butter
8 cups toasted bread, cubed
1 cup onion, chopped
1 cup celery, chopped
1/2 pound bulk sausage
2 tablespoons chopped fresh parsley
1 teaspoon fresh sage leaves, minced
1 cup chicken broth
1/2 teaspoon fresh sweet marjoram, minced
1/2 teaspoon fresh thyme, minced
1/4 teaspoon freshly ground black pepper
1 teaspoon poultry seasoning
salt to taste

Melt the butter in a large skillet and sauté the onion and celery until transparent. Brown the sausage in a separate skillet until cooked through. Add all the above to the bread cubes and mix lightly. Add the herbs and seasonings and the chicken broth. Toss lightly. Add more stock if a moister stuffing is desired. This recipe is enough to stuff a twelve pound turkey.

VEGETABLE MEDLEY

1 teaspoon rosemary
1 1/2 teaspoons sage
1 1/2 teaspoons marjoram
1 1/2 teaspoons summer savory
pinch cayenne
freshly ground black pepper
2 cloves garlic, crushed
1/2 cup olive oil
cauliflower
carrots
pea pods
green beans

Mix the herbs and seasonings together with the olive oil well and let stand overnight at room temperature. Prepare the vegetables in serving-size pieces and cook until al dente. Add the sauce, blend well and serve.

A MENU FOR NOVEMBER

Curried Coriander Soup

Honey Cakes

Brown Rice Salad

Vegetables Pie with Fines Herbes

Spiced Squash

Gingerbread

CURRIED CORIANDER SOUP

2 tablespoons butter
1 teaspoon ground coriander
1/2 teaspoon ground cumin
2 tablespoons flour
3 3/4 cups chicken broth, heated
juice of 1/2 lemon
dash black pepper
2/3 cup light cream
1/3 cup cooked rice

Heat the butter in a saucepan and stir in the ground coriander and cumin. Stir over low heat for 1 minute, then add the flour. Stir for 2 minutes, then add the heated stock. Stir until blended and simmer for 4 minutes. Add the lemon juice and pepper. Stir in the cream and the cooked rice and heat. Serve with croutons.

HONEY CAKES

1 cup milk, scalded
1/4 cup butter
1/3 cup honey
1 package yeast
1/4 cup warm water
1 teaspoon salt
5 cups flour
2 large eggs

Add the butter and honey to the scalded milk and stir until the butter melts. Dissolve the yeast in the warm water and add to the cooled milk mixture. Add the salt and 2 cups of the flour. Blend in the eggs and the remaining flour to form a soft dough. Place in a buttered bowl, cover, and let rise until doubled in bulk. Shape into rolls and place on a greased cookie sheet. Cover and let rise again. Bake at 400 degrees for 20 minutes, or until done.

BROWN RICE SALAD

8 cups cooked brown rice
1 red onion, minced
1 green pepper, diced
1 cup celery, thinly sliced
1 large carrot, grated
1 cup cabbage, finely shredded
1 large tomato, diced
1/3 cup finely chopped fresh parsley
2 cups peas, lightly steamed
1 tablespoon curry powder
1/4 cup mayonnaise
1/4 cup olive oil
1/4 cup herb vinegar
1 tablespoon Dijon mustard
3 cloves garlic, minced

Combine the rice with all the vegetables and the parsley. Mix in the curry powder and the mayonnaise.
Blend the olive oil, vinegar, Dijon mustard, and garlic to make the dressing. Pour it over the salad, and toss well. Makes 12 servings.

VEGETABLE PIE WITH FINES HERBES

2 cups broccoli*
1 cup peas*
1 cup green beans*
1/2 cup chopped onion
1/2 cup chopped green pepper
1 cup shredded cheddar cheese
1 cup milk
3/4 cup Bisquick mix
3 eggs
1 teaspoon salt
1/4 teaspoon pepper
1 tablespoon Fines Herbes
fresh tomato for garnish

*Cook for 5 minutes if frozen.

Lightly grease a 9" pie pan. Mix vegetables, onion, green pepper and cheese in pie plate. Beat together remaining ingredients until smooth. Pour into the pie plate. Bake until golden brown at 400 degrees, about 35 minutes. Garnish with a slice of fresh tomato.

SPICED SQUASH

1 medium butternut squash
3 tablespoons butter
1/4 cup sugar
1 teaspoon cinnamon

Peel, cube and cook the squash until tender. Drain and mash thoroughly. Add the butter and a blend of the sugar and the cinnamon. Beat well together.

GINGER BREAD

1/2 cup softened butter
1/2 cup sugar
1 egg, beaten
1 cup molasses
2 1/2 cups flour
1 1/2 teaspoons soda
1 teaspoon cinnamon
1 teaspoon ginger
1/2 teaspoon cloves
1/2 teaspoon salt
1 cup hot water

Cream the butter and sugar. Add the egg and molasses. Sift and add the flour, soda, cinnamon, ginger, cloves and salt. Add the hot water and beat until smooth. Pour into greased 8" square pan. Bake at 325 degrees for 35 minutes. Top with whipped cream and a bit of candied ginger.

DECEMBER

Christmas comes but once a year
and when it comes it brings good cheer
a pocketful of money and a cellarful of beer
and a good fat pig to last you all the year.

St. Lucia's Day is December 13, which celebrates the Festival of Light, the Winter Solstice. St. Lucia was especially venerated by those people living where winter nights arc very long and dark.

In Swedish homes today, the youngest daughter is chosen to be the Lucia queen. She arises early, and wearing a white gown and a crown of lighted candles, brings breakfast and a song to members of her household and to the animals on the farm. We were surprised indeed when our daughter Wendy, woke us early on this day to carry out the tradition!

St. Nicholas was the patron saint of sailors, travelers, bakers, merchants and especially children. An old legend tells of his giving gold to each of three girls who had no dowries, and thus were unable to marry. St. Nicholas' day is December 6, and much of Europe still celebrates this special day.

The Dutch brought the "Visit of St. Nicholas" to America; the name "Santa Claus" comes from Sinter Klass, Dutch for St. Nicholas.

Bring the fresh scents of evergreens in for holiday decorating! Mistletoe, the plant of peace, banishes evil spirits and protects homes against thunder and lightening. Holly protects against witches and the evil eye. Rosemary signifies remembrance and friendship. Laurel protects and purifies, and is symbolic of victory, distinction and honor.

Christmas festivities signal the culmination of our labors throughout the year. Decorating for this beloved holiday is a joyful task! A fragrant tree is cut and stands in one corner of the dining room. It is brought in on the first of December so that it can be enjoyed by our luncheon guests throughout the month. Our tree decorations are handmade: cornhusk angels, handcarved doves, cinnamon sticks tied with bright red ribbons, strings of red wooden beads, and chains made from woodchips.

Fresh evergreens and laurel from the woods nearby are placed about with abandon – on the mantle and windowsills and tucked into cupboards. Red candles in tin candleholders brighten tables and a Swedish straw buk stands under the tree.

A wooden shoe is placed on the mantle to honor St. Nicholas. In this, we place a branch of broom plant to represent Black Peter's switches, teasel to represent the cloth merchants, and yellow tansy to represent the bags of gold St. Nicholas gave to charity.

Close your eyes and imagine the pungent odors of orange and spice of the pomander, the sweet scents of roses and lavender and other ingredients of the winter potpourri, the woodsmoke from the fireplace and the wonderful spicy aromas from the kitchen!

Christmas – a time for family and friends, inspiration, and a look back over the blessings of the year.

ROSEMARY

Tender Perennial
rosmarinus officinalis

Rosemary is an evergreen shrub growing from three to six feet tall. Rosemary is a native of the Mediterranean, and its name means "dew of the sea" – it has a great love for salt air, sun and dew. Its needle-like leaves vary from grey-green to dark green.

Rosmarinus prostratus is a creeping, blue flowering variety, and is lovely when planted in a hanging pot.

All rosemarys prefer sunny locations. The plant cannot stand heavy frosts, and is best potted in a large pot which can be sunk in the ground and then is easily brought in for the winter months. Inside, the foliage must be sprayed with water every day or two to supply a humid atmosphere. Its roots must not be allowed to dehydrate, or the plant will die. Rosemary requires evenly moist, well-drained soil that is alkaline. It should be fertilized several times during its active growing season. Seeds are slow to germinate. Rosemary can be started easily from cuttings: take a 6" tip of new growth and bury its lower 4" in sand or vermiculite.

To dry rosemary, cut the branches before the plant begins flowering. Hang in bunches in a shady, airy spot. When dry, strip the needles from the branches and store in airtight containers.

Rosemary has long had the reputation for having the ability to improve the memory, and was a symbol of constancy. Sprigs of the plant were woven into bridal bouquets and given to wedding guests. A sentimental herb, rosemary was planted on graves throughout history.

Legend has ascribed the blue flowers of the rosemary to the Virgin Mary. So the story goes, the Holy family stopped to rest during their flight from Egypt and Mary draped her blue robe over a white-blooming rosemary bush. From that day on, the plant's flowers have been blue in her honor.

Rosemary can often be found in cosmetics, soaps, and hair tonics. It makes a very pleasant incense when burned; or simmer a handful of crushed rosemary in a pan of water.

A sprig of rosemary makes a pleasant bookmark! Dried sprays of rosemary can be used to repel moths in closets.

Rosemary is highly valued as a seasoner for beef, pork, lamb or poultry. It can be added to soups, stuffings or made into jelly. It is an excellent addition to herb breads.

A vigorous rosemary plant in the garden means the woman of the house heads the household! Rosemary is best known as a symbol of remembrance, friendship and love.

Marinades, salad dressings and cream sauces all benefit from rosemary's robust character. Crush or mince the spiky leaves before sprinkling over or rubbing into foods. Use rosemary to flavor baked potatoes, or to make an herb butter for vegetables. The large stems from mature plants can be used as barbecue skewers!

In some Mediterranean villages, linen is spread over rosemary to dry so that the sun will extract its moth-repellent aroma.

ZUCCHINI WITH ROSEMARY

1 pound zucchini, thinly sliced
1 tomato, chopped
1 small onion, finely chopped
2 teaspoons finely chopped fresh rosemary
2 tablespoons vegetable oil

Heat the oil in a saucepan and add the remaining ingredients.
Cover and simmer gently until soft, stirring frequently.

ROSEMARY BREAD

1 package dry yeast
2 tablespoons finely snipped fresh rosemary
1 cup warm water
1/4 cup butter, melted
1/2 teaspoon sugar
1 teaspoon salt
1 cup whole wheat flour
2 1/2 cups white flour

In a large bowl, sprinkle yeast and 1 tablespoon rosemary over
the warm water. Let stand until bubbly, about 10 minutes. Stir
in the sugar, salt, whole wheat flour and 3/4 cup white flour.
Beat well. Gradually beat in 1 1/2 cups white flour to made a
stiff dough. Turn out and knead about 10 minutes, adding more
flour if necessary. Place dough in a greased bowl, turning to
coat all sides. Cover and let rise until doubled, about 1 hour.
Punch down dough. Turn out and gently knead for 10 strokes.
Shape into a loaf and place in a greased 8" x 4" loaf pan. Brush
top of loaf with melted butter. Let rise until doubled, about 1
hour. Brush loaf again with melted butter and sprinkle with
remaining 1 tablespoon rosemary. Bake at 375 degrees about 45
minutes. Cool completely on a rack.

BAKED CHICKEN WITH LEMON AND ROSEMARY

1 tablespoon fresh rosemary, chopped
juice and rind of 1 lemon
1/2 cup white wine
1 teaspoon chopped garlic
4 chicken breasts

Marinate the chicken in the above mixture overnight. Bake at 350 degrees for 1 hour or more. Baste often with the marinade.

CARROTS AU GRATIN WITH ROSEMARY

3 cups sliced carrots, cooked
1 10 3/4-ounce can cream of celery soup
1 cup shredded cheddar cheese
1 tablespoon fresh parsley, chopped
1 tablespoon snipped fresh rosemary
1/4 cup dry bread crumbs
1 tablespoon butter, melted

Butter a 1 quart casserole. In medium bowl, combine carrots, soup, and cheese. Pour into prepared casserole. In a small bowl combine bread crumbs and butter. Sprinkle over the carrots. Bake at 350 degrees for 25 minutes. Garnish with fresh rosemary.

ROSEMARY PUNCH

1 large can pineapple juice
5 teaspoons fresh rosemary
1 1/2 cups lemon juice
2 cups water
fresh lemon slices and rosemary sprigs
1 large bottle ginger ale

Boil 1 cup of pineapple juice with the rosemary. Remove from heat and let stand 5 minutes, then strain and cool. Add all other ingredients except the ginger ale. Pour into a punch bowl over ice and add ginger ale just before serving. Float lemon slices and rosemary sprigs in a punch bowl.

Hint: Add rosemary sprigs to an ice ring for a taste treat.

ROSEMARY HERB BUTTER

1/4 pound butter
1 clove garlic, minced
1 teaspoon lemon juice
2 tablespoons fresh rosemary, minced

Cream the butter. Blend in the garlic, lemon juice and rosemary. Allow to mellow for a day or two. This butter can be refrigerated for up to one month. Try it on grilled meats!

CRISPY ROSEMARY POTATOES

2 large baking potatoes, peeled
1/4 cup butter, melted
black pepper
6 sprigs fresh rosemary, finely snipped

Preheat oven to 350 degrees. Slice the potatoes 1/2" thick and quarter the slices. Place in a single layer on a baking sheet and brush with 1/2 the melted butter. Sprinkle with 1/2 the rosemary and pepper. Bake until golden, about 15 minutes. Turn the slices over, brush with the remaining butter, then sprinkle with remaining rosemary. Bake until crisp and golden, about 15 more minutes. Serve immediately.

AUNT DAISY'S MOLASSES COOKIES

1/2 cup shortening
1/2 cup sugar
1 cup molasses
1/2 cup hot water
1 teaspoon soda
1/2 teaspoon nutmeg
1/2 teaspoon cinnamon
1/2 teaspoon vanilla
4 cups flour

Cream the shortening and the sugar. Add the molasses and the hot water. Stir in the vanilla; combine the dry ingredients and work in, adding more flour if necessary to make a stiff dough. Roll out 1/2" thick and cut into rounds. Bake at 400 degrees for 8 minutes.

KAHLUA

4 cups sugar
3 cups water
1 cup boiling water
1/2 cup instant coffee
1 vanilla bean
1 quart vodka

Bring sugar and 3 cups water to a boil and continue boiling for 20 minutes. The mixture will become syrupy. Cool. Combine the 1 cup boiling water with the instant coffee. Split the vanilla bean lengthwise and drop it into 1/2 gallon jug. Pour the vodka over the bean, then add the syrup and coffee mixtures. Let Kahlua age for weeks, covered.

A MENU FOR DECEMBER

Holiday Cheese Log

White Pepper Potato Soup

St. Lucia Buns

Crab Casserole

Broccoli in Dill Sauce

Christmas Brownies

Wassail

HOLIDAY CHEESE LOG

1 8-ounce package cream cheese, softened
2 ounces blue cheese, crumbled
4 ounces sharp cheddar cheese, shredded
1/4 cup finely chopped onion
1 tablespoon Worcestershire Sauce
1 tablespoon lemon juice
3/4 cup chopped pecans
1/2 cup finely chopped fresh parsley

Combine all the ingredients except the pecans and parsley.
Beat for 2 minutes on medium speed. Stir in 1/4 cup pecans.
Cover and chill 1 hour or until firm. Spread chopped parsley
and pecans evenly on a sheet of waxed paper. Form chilled
mixture into log shape, and roll in parsley and pecans. Wrap
and chill for several hours. Serve with crackers or thinly sliced
rye bread.

WHITE PEPPER POTATO SOUP

4 large potatoes
2 large onions
1/2 teaspoon herb salt
1 1/4 cups water
1 quart milk
1 pint heavy cream
3 tablespoons flour
1/4 pound butter cut into small pieces
1/2 teaspoon white pepper
2 tablespoons vegetables flakes
1 teaspoon dried chives
1 tablespoon parsley
1/2 teaspoon garlic powder
1/2 teaspoon paprika
fresh parsley

Peel and cube potatoes and onions. Add salt and 1 cup water and simmer until tender. Drain off water, add milk and cream. Mix flour and 1/4 cup cold water to a thin paste, add to soup, and simmer on low heat until thickened. Add the pepper, vegetable flakes, chives, parsley and garlic powder. Pour into hot soup bowls. Dot with a piece of butter and sprinkle with paprika and parsley.

ST. LUCIA BUNS

2 packages dry yeast
1/2 cup warm water
1 cup warm milk
1/4 cup honey
1 teaspoon ground cardamon
pinch of saffron
1 1/2 teaspoons salt
1/2 cup butter
2 eggs
6-7 cups flour
raisins
1 egg white

Combine yeast and warm water. In a large bowl, combine milk, honey, spices, and salt. Add butter, eggs and the yeast mixture. Beat in enough flour for a stiff dough. Turn onto a lightly floured board and knead 10 minutes. Place in a greased bowl, cover and let rise until doubled. Turn out again and knead for 3 minutes. Return to bowl, cover and let rise again for 45 minutes. Turn out, punch down and knead for 5 minutes. Cover with a towel and let rest for 15 minutes. Divide dough into 24 pieces and roll each piece into a rope about 12" long. Place on a greased baking sheet and coil it into an S-shape. Place a raisin in the center of each roll. Brush tops lightly with egg white and sprinkle with sugar. Bake at 350 degrees for 15-20 minutes.

CRAB CASSEROLE

1/2 cup butter
1 teaspoon Worcestershire Sauce
1 teaspoon parsley flakes
1 pound crabmeat
1 8-ounce package cream cheese
1/2 teaspoon celery seed
2 teaspoons lemon juice
4 ounces mozzarella cheese, grated
1/2 cup grated parmesan cheese
1 tablespoon Fines Herbes
paprika

Melt the butter, add the cream cheese and blend. Add the celery seed, Worcestershire, parsley, lemon juice and fines herbes. Stir in the mozzarella cheese and the crabmeat. Turn into a 2 quart casserole and sprinkle with parmesan cheese and paprika. Bake at 350 degrees for 45 minutes.

BROCCOLI IN DILL SAUCE

1 bunch broccoli
1 tablespoon prepared mustard
1/4 teaspoon dill seed

Cook the broccoli just until tender. Drain. Combine the mustard and dill and serve over the broccoli.

CHRISTMAS BROWNIES

2/3 cup butter
4 squares (ounces) chocolate
4 eggs
2 cups sugar
2 teaspoons vanilla
1 1/2 cups cake flour
1 teaspoon baking powder
2 cups chopped walnuts
confectioners sugar

Melt the butter with the chocolate. Beat the eggs, add the sugar gradually, then add vanilla and chocolate. Stir in the flour and baking powder, then add the nuts. Spread in 9" x 9" pan, well greased. Bake at 325 degrees for 30 minutes. Cut into squares and roll in confectioners sugar.

CHRISTMAS WASSAIL

2 quarts apple cider
juice of 2 lemons
4 cups orange juice
4 2-inch sticks of cinnamon
2 tablespoons whole cloves
2 tablespoons ground allspice
1/4 tablespoon grated nutmeg
1 cup sugar

Bring the cider to a boil. In a separate pot, mix the remaining ingredients and bring to a boil. Simmer for 10 minutes. Combine cider and fruit syrup and strain. Bring to a boil again and serve hot.

RECIPE INDEX

PICKITY PLACE

Since its opening in 1975, Pickity Place, in Mason, NH, has become a mecca for herb lovers far and wide. Renowned for its five-course herbal lunchs, customers search out this rural 1786 cottage to enjoy its peaceful ambiance and delicious herb-kissed foods devised by Judy Walter.